EVERY PRECIOUS STONE

The Building of New City Fellowship

"This is the Lord's doing;
it is marvelous in our eyes."

Every Precious Stone–The Building of New City Fellowship

Copyright ©2018 by The Mark and Linda Belz Trust

ISBN 9781790864645

All rights reserved. No part of this publication may be reproduced, stored in a retrieval system, or transmitted in any form or by any means – electronic, mechanical, photocopy, recording, or any other – except for brief quotations in printed reviews, without the prior permission of the publisher.

Any internet addresses (websites, blogs, etc.) and telephone numbers in this book are offered only as resources. They are not meant as our endorsements.

All Scripture quotations, unless otherwise indicated, are taken from The Holy Bible, English Standard Version® (ESV®) Copyright © 2001 by Crossway, a publishing ministry of Good News Publishers. All rights reserved. ESV Text Edition: 2011.

Editor: Linda E. Belz

Design and production: Nat Belz, BooksBrothers

Front cover art: Greg MacNair

Rear cover calligraphy: Theresa Kragnes

Replicas of front cover art and rear cover calligraphy, suitable for framing, are available from publisher.

BOOKSBROTHERS PRESS
15 WESTCHESTER DRIVE
ASHEVILLE, NC 28803

In memory of Rudy and Collyn Schmidt

Acknowledgements

I HAVE NEVER WRITTEN A HISTORY of anything or anybody prior to this effort. I now find that adequately acknowledging everyone who helps in compiling historical material is difficult if not impossible. There are so many people who have given time for interviews, have checked and re-checked drafts, looked for documents, or answered my emails and telephone calls just to assure a level of accuracy. To each of those not named here, I express my great appreciation for your time, your work, and your willingness to bear with me.

There are some who have helped in exceptional ways. The history of New City goes back into the early 1960s, and many of those involved in its beginnings are now in heaven. But two special people are still here. One is Will Barker, who preached a pivotal sermon on Christians and race relations in 1963, and helped start up the work of Third Street Sunday School in Chattanooga, the children's ministry that evolved into New City Fellowship. Will has given much of his time and many valuable papers to provide information and documentation for the earliest stages of New City's history.

I wish that Rudy and Collyn Schmidt could have been consulted, but they had died before this project began. They were two of a trio of originators of Third Street Sunday School. The third member, however, was Arline Wetzel Cadwell, who is still here with us, is still worshiping at NCF Chattanooga, and remembers details about the 1968 inauguration of the tiny mission at the foot of Lookout Mountain in Chattanooga. I doubt that this book could have gotten off the ground without Arline's time and patient help.

Vera Parkin, who is always too busy as a musician with the St. Louis Symphony Orchestra and as a piano teacher, enthusiastically volunteered to do interviews of several people involved in New City Fellowship St. Louis. Her interviews were detailed and accurate, and displayed her enthusiasm for Kingdom work.

I am thankful for the work of Greg MacNair, who did an original oil painting for the cover art,[1] and did it beautifully. Thanks also is appropriate to Theresa Kragnes, who in 1978 allowed me to purchase her calligraphy of Isaiah 58:6-9 and has given permission to use it on the back cover of this book. In the law firm that I was associated with for more than 30 years, Theresa's calligraphy hung in the reception room as a testimony to clients and a reminder to members of the firm as to what it had adopted as its primary reason for existence. In my estimation it also summarizes much of New City Fellowship's reason for existence.

MY DEEPEST THANKS goes to my wife Linda, not just because she's been patient and encouraging as I worked on my laptop day and night, nor just because she's been a loving companion for 53 years, nor because she is a writer far superior to her husband, nor because she's edited this book numerous times. All of those are true, but my deep appreciation for her with regard to this effort is that she sensed from about 1970, long before I did, that New City was something special. She saw (or heard) something wonderfully exciting in their music, particularly that of James Ward, and helped me to step out of my stiff classical music box so that I learned to love it as well. I still love classical, so haven't lost a thing. She was also much more aware of and concerned about

---

[1] Greg's art is an adaptation of New City's original "logo" created by Doreen Kellogg in the very early days of New City Fellowship Chattanooga.

racial issues than I was in the 1970s, and her heart for the poor led her to volunteer at Jubilee School in North St. Louis, associated with Murphy Blair Community Church which we joined. It was during that time that we concluded that St. Louis was in dire need of a Chattanooga-style NCF ministry. Our prayers were answered in 1991 when Barry and Ann Henning agreed to come from New City in Chattanooga to start a New City in St. Louis.

Linda has been partially incapacitated for many years with an auto-immune disease that has made attendance at New City St. Louis difficult. But her heart and mind have consistently been there, thanks especially to some dear New City friends—among them, Darwin White, Rosalind Alexander and Sandra Clay.

CONTENTS

Introduction 7

I. *A Surprise, A Murder and A Sermon (1963)* 11

II. *Wilmington Synod (1968)* 25

III. *Third Street Sunday School* 33

IV. *Randy & Joan* 39

V. *New City Fellowship, Chattanooga* 53

VI. *The Songmaker* 83

VII. *Barry & Ann* 93

VIII. *New City Fellowship, St. Louis* 105

IX. *New City Network* 145

X. *The State of the Church* 155

XI. *Afterthought: Precious Stones* 165

APPENDIX I: *Core Values* 171

APPENDIX II: *Is An Integrated Church Possible?* 179

INTRODUCTION

JESUS PROMISED, "ON THIS ROCK I WILL BUILD MY CHURCH." He said this to his disciples after Peter uttered the great confession, "You are the Christ, the Son of the Living God."

In congregational meetings when we discuss building a church, we're typically speaking of a comprehensive program: hiring an architect, initiating a capital funds campaign, obtaining necessary financing, engaging a contractor, and all the rest that goes into constructing a suitable physical *building* for fellowship and worship. We drive by the site repeatedly, watching with excitement as we see the footings placed, the framework rise, the roof topped off, the siding, the interior drywall, the windows, the offices and classrooms. We must go inside to tour the sanctuary. It is there that we expect for the next many years to be singing together, hearing God's word preached, eating at the Lord's Table, announcing our faith in unison as we recite the Apostle's Creed, and praying together. It is in the sanctuary that we will be worshiping with one another as the Body of Christ.

The significance of the physical aspect of the New Testament church is often downplayed, and understandably so. The Church that Jesus told his disciples he is building is spiritual, not physical: "[Y]ou yourselves like living stones are being built up as a spiritual house, to be a holy priesthood, to offer spiritual sacrifices acceptable to God through Jesus Christ" (1 Pet. 2:5).[2] The

---

[2] It is significant that this "living stones" passage was written by Simon Peter, whom the Lord was addressing immediately after Peter's great confession. Jesus said to Peter, "On this rock I will build my church, and the gates of hell shall not prevail against it" (Mt. 16:18). Most reformed theologians agree that the "rock" is not Simon Peter, but his confession: "You

building for this Church is not constructed of stones dug from a quarry, but of living stones.

Yet, much like the tabernacle was for the Israelites, our physical building is a picture of God's spiritual house. As we watch our congregation's new building being constructed, stone upon stone, brick upon brick, we are witnessing a physical image of a spiritual reality. The spiritual reality is that Jesus is the architect and builder of the true Church. His children are the material he uses. We are privileged to see *ourselves* being built—amazingly—into the house in which he intends to dwell for all eternity.[3]

In this book I have taken a look at some of the stones the Lord has used, and is using, to build New City Fellowship. Not all NCF stones are mentioned here, because there are thousands of them, and the ones named in this book may not be the most important ones. In fact, in God's view no one stone is more important than another. Each one of them, whether mentioned in the following pages or not, is not merely important but actually indispensable.[4] Some may just be more *visible* than others. But every stone is precious and beautiful in the "new city" the Lord is building:

> Afflicted city, lashed by storms and not comforted,
>   I will rebuild you with stones of turquoise,
>   your foundations with lapis lazuli.

---

are the Christ, the Son of the Living God." John Calvin wrote: "Peter, in his own and his brethren's name, had confessed that Christ was the Son of God [Mt. 16:16]. Upon this rock Christ builds his church. For there is but one foundation, as Paul says, apart from which no other can be laid [1 Cor. 3:11]." Calvin, John, *Institutes of the Christian Religion*, ed. John T. McNeill, trans. Ford Lewis Battles. 2 vols. Louisville KY: Westminster Press, 1960, IV,vi,3, p.1107.

[3] In the apocalyptic vision, John states: "[The beast] opened its mouth to utter blasphemies against God, blaspheming his name and *his dwelling, that is, those who dwell in heaven.*" (Rev. 13:6) (emphasis added).

[4] "The eye cannot say to the hand, 'I don't need you!' And the head cannot say to the feet, 'I don't need you!' On the contrary, those parts of the body that seem to be weaker are indispensable." (1 Cor. 12:21-22).

> I will make your battlements of rubies,
>   your gates of sparkling jewels,
>   and all your walls of precious stones.
> All your children will be taught by the Lord,
>   and great will be their peace. (Isa. 54:11-13)

I could be faulted for centering the subject matter of this book primarily on Chattanooga, Tennessee, and St. Louis, Missouri. Obviously, there are many other locations that deserve consideration. But these two hubs are important historically, because NCF originated in Chattanooga, and about 25 years later NCF St. Louis became its first 'offshoot.' From 1992 on, virtually all other churches and ministries now connected with NCF have sprung from, or been significantly influenced by, these two centers of ministry.

I could also be faulted, and probably will be, for mentioning the names and frequently the brief bios of New City participants especially visible to me. I have tried to go beyond that circle, but any individual's vision is limited, and often skewed. Thus the reader should consider the people named and described here not as exhaustive but only illustrative.

I would also urge readers to consider the significance of the stories behind the names. The story of how a person was raised, came to know Jesus, was educated, became interested in the church, and was brought to a particular field of service in Kingdom work is instructive as to the manner in which the Lord selects, chisels and burnishes the stones he uses to construct his Church—his one true, eternal, yet invisible home.

Some years back I was asked to teach an adult education class on Paul's letter to the Romans. About two weeks into the class I looked around at the 20 or so folks in attendance and realized that I knew almost nothing of their histories. I didn't know how they came to Christ; I had never heard about all the twists and turns that resulted in their ending up on such and such a Sunday morning in an adult education class on the Book of Romans.

There were stories behind those faces. So I decided to allocate 15 minutes at the start of each class for testimonies. For the ten weeks remaining, we heard about their journeys. We had more volunteers than we had Sundays, and it was an amazing experience. The scheme fit right in with what we were studying because the Book of Romans has a whole lot to say about the sovereignty of God in salvation, and hearing individual histories proved to be exciting and encouraging, as we witnessed God's sovereign plan of salvation fleshed out in real people, in real time and space.

No matter what church you're a part of, whether New City or otherwise, your story needs to be told. Others will be edified and encouraged. And we should listen to the stories of one another. It will help us to understand something of what the Builder's objectives are, and how he goes about achieving them.

IT WASN'T PLANNED THIS WAY, but it happens that this short history of New City Fellowship is being published almost exactly 50 years after the church began. It was in the summer of 1968 that Third Street Sunday School first met in Chattanooga, Tennessee. The intervening half century between then and now displays how the Lord has used little kids, untrained preachers, bathtubs, financial catastrophes, unanswered mail, flip charts, war, failed ministries, chance meetings, misunderstandings, rock 'n roll, depression, nosebleeds and a host of other strange things that you and I wouldn't dream of using to build a church. Most likely, the Lord will continue to employ that strategy for the next 50 years. We must just keep watching.

1.

A SURPRISE, A MURDER AND A SERMON
(1963)

"If race means something to any of us, it is evidence that Christ has not come to mean enough."—WILLIAM S. BARKER, 1963

WILL BARKER was called as pastor of Hazelwood Reformed Presbyterian Church in suburban St. Louis, Missouri, in 1960. Born and raised in St. Louis, it was his home turf. He had graduated Princeton University with a B.A. in history in 1956, earned his Masters at Cornell in 1957 and believed he was called to the ministry. He narrowed his seminary options to two: Westminster in Philadelphia and Covenant in St. Louis. He chose Covenant, earned his Masters of Divinity there in 1960, was ordained, and installed that summer as pastor at Hazelwood.[5] He job as pastor was part-time because he also taught history at Covenant College.

Hazelwood was a church plant of the Reformed Presbyterian Church, Columbus Synod. At first, it was peopled mostly by students and faculty from Covenant College and Seminary, which shared a campus in St. Louis County at the time.

---

[5] Barker would later serve as Moderator of the Reformed Presbyterian Church, Evangelical Synod (1973) and as Moderator of the Presbyterian Church in America (1994).

The congregation met for some years in a Hazelwood florist shop, but though the place had a pleasant aroma and worked well for weddings and funerals, they soon recognized the need to build a permanent sanctuary. They looked at several properties and bought a tract of land in Hazelwood not far from the St. Louis airport, then called Lambert Field.

A Surprise

After title to the property had been transferred and construction begun, Will Barker drove to the St. Louis County recorder's office to look at the deed to the property they had already purchased. A woman in the recorder's office brought him a copy of the recorded deed, and Will, historian and scholar that he was, read it all the way through. It looked fine, but did make reference to the property's being "subject to any covenants of record," and so Will thought he should check on that too. He asked the woman if she could rustle up "any covenants" affecting the property. She complied, found one such covenant, and Will read that all the way through too. He was surprised to find this provision:

> Each of the parties of the First Part covenants and agrees and does hereby create, establish and attach to his, her or its lands herein above described, or his, her or its interest therein, the following [restriction] upon the use, occupation and enjoyment, sale, alienation (voluntary or by operation of law), encumbrance and descent of said lands, or any part thereof, or any interest therein, and does agree that neither he, she or it…shall or will at any time within the period hereinafter mentioned… *[s]ell, convey, lease or rent to a Negro or Negroes, or deliver possession to or permit to be occupied by a Negro or Negroes* (no matter how the right to occupancy or title shall be attempted to be acquired) any of the said parcels of land belonging to par-

ties of the First Part and herein above described, or any part thereof or any interest therein.[6] (emphasis added)

Will was not only surprised, but dismayed. This didn't sound like a clause Hazelwood Reformed Presbyterian Church would want in its chain of title. But because Hazelwood RPC had already accepted and recorded the deed, the odious restriction was already there. Among other things it meant that if the church ever sought to sell the property, it couldn't sell it to blacks. That didn't quite coordinate with what Will had studied at Covenant Theological Seminary, or what he knew to be right. Most importantly, it didn't square with scripture.[7]

Will mulled this over in his mind. What would it be like to canvass in a neighborhood where African Americans were excluded? What would the witness of his church be? Would the people of Hazelwood Reformed Presbyterian Church welcome those of another race and color if they did happen to come? Would the community at large give the church a hard time if they did? The answers to those questions were largely unknown to Will, but the issues couldn't be ignored. At least Hazelwood RPC had to

---

[6] This kind of "restrictive covenant" was typical in urban and suburban areas throughout the United States from 1917 until 1968. Often such covenants excluded Jews as well as blacks. In 1917 the United States Supreme Court, in *Buchanan vs. Warley*, held that state laws and municipal ordinances requiring segregation in housing were void, as a violation of the Fourteenth Amendment to the Constitution. Restrictive covenants were efforts to bypass *Buchanan vs. Warley*, by providing "protection" for white communities in a private but legal manner and were not finally abolished until Congress passed the "Fair Housing Act" in 1968, declaring all such restrictive covenants void and unenforceable.

[7] The principle of racial equality is embedded in Old Testament law. For example, equal treatment for the alien was a requirement: "You shall treat the stranger who sojourns with you as the native among you, and you shall love him as yourself, for you were strangers in the land of Egypt: I am the LORD your God" (Lev. 19:34). This "equal protection" principle is repeated multiple times in the Old Testament, which is perhaps one of the reasons it was enshrined in the Fifth and Fourteenth Amendments to the U.S. Constitution.

know where it stood, take a position, and have a clear witness in the community consistent with its position.

During this time, Will and his wife Gail were busy—not only with the new congregation but also with Covenant College where Will was teaching. He had to prepare a sermon and a week of lectures at the same time. The race issue did have to be addressed, however, not just because of the restrictive covenant down at the county recorder's office, but also because in the early 60's it was a pressing issue all across America. Regrettably, many white politically conservative evangelical Christians were outspoken in those days in their opposition to integration, and many others didn't know where they stood on race issues, where they should stand, or whether it even mattered. Will scheduled a sermon on the topic for June 16, 1963.

A Murder

Medgar Evers was an African American who served in the United States Army during World War II. He later earned his B.A. in business administration at what is now Alcorn State University. Then, the same year that the United States Supreme Court decided the famed *Brown vs. Board of Education* case (1954),[8] Evers applied for admission to the University of Mississippi Law School. He was denied entry because he was African-American.

Evers became increasingly active in the Civil Rights movement. He was particularly active in still-segregated Mississippi, serving as a field secretary for the National Association for the Advancement of Colored People (NAACP). He, his wife Myrlie and their children maintained a home in Jackson, Mississippi.

Naturally, like Martin Luther King, Jr., Evers was hated by the Klan and other white supremacists. One dark day the hatred

---

[8] In *Brown*, the Court ruled 9-0 that the former "separate but equal" doctrine approving separate public schools for blacks and whites was unconstitutional, stating that "separate educational facilities are inherently unequal." *Brown vs. Board of Education of Topeka*, 347 U.S. 483 (1954).

bore its evil fruit.⁹ On June 12, 1963, as Evers was returning to his home from a morning meeting, a member of the Klan gunned him down with a high-powered rifle from across the street. Evers died an hour later.

The man who was finally convicted of the murder—in 1994, thirty-one years after the killing—was Byron De La Beckwith. In addition to holding membership in the Klan, De La Beckwith was a member of the "Citizens' Council," which vigorously opposed any form of integration.¹⁰ De La Beckwith heard what they had to say; he listened to their 'preaching,' adopted their racist thinking as his own and decided to take action—to do something about what he now believed. He became an active racist, and Evers' murder was the tragic consequence.

A Sermon

It had been just four days since Medgar Evers was murdered in Jackson. On Sunday morning June 16 Will Barker preached his sermon in Hazelwood. As we shall see, that sermon was used by the Lord, in his sovereign providence, to help bring New City Fellowship into existence.

Will had decided to preach a series of topical sermons that summer on current issues facing the church, and this topic was first on the list. Of course the Medgar Evers death came as a shock to the world, but providentially provided a stark and poi-

---

⁹ Gen. 4:3-8; 1 Jn. 3:15.

¹⁰ White "Citizens' Councils" were prevalent throughout the south during that time and officially held to a policy of non-violence, unlike the Klan. They were, however, openly racist. Many members of the Southern Presbyterian Church, including elders and clergy, were members of these Citizens' Councils. Historian Sean Lucas writes that in 1957, the session of First Presbyterian Church, Jackson MS, a leading congregation in the formation of the Presbyterian Church in America in 1973, defended these Citizens' Groups thus: "This session would point out that there are numerous citizens' councils and groups which are composed of Christian citizens of the highest type…" Lucas, Sean Michael, *For a Continuing Church*, p.120. Phillipsburg, NJ: P&R Publishing (2015).

gnant rebuke to America and particularly to the church as to where it stood on racial issues.

Fifty-three years later, this author asked Barker if he remembered much about his 1963 sermon. The historian and scholar came through: he had kept his notes! And they proved to be much more than notes. At the top of these hand-written notes is the memo "HAZELWOOD—SUN A.M.—6-16-63." Here are Barker's notes, verbatim:[11]

Our Brother or Our Neighbor
Acts 17:16-31

INTRODUCTION

The shooting of Medgar Evers, Field Representative for the NAACP (National Association for the Advancement of Colored People), in his own driveway in Jackson, Mississippi, has shocked people 'round the world. Yet it is no surprise to any of us in America, for as long as any of us has lived, we have been aware of prejudice against the Negro, and the Bible says that "whosoever hateth his brother is a murderer." This hatred has existed in the hearts of many Americans for years. What saddens me is that this discrimination is manifested especially through the "Bible Belt," where people claim, as we do, to believe the Bible as God's Word. Yet this feeling is not confined to the South. In the North, office clerks have been told by their employer not to bother filing applications for African-American people, and housing restorations have limited where Negroes can reside in this free country. The very ground on which this church in Hazelwood sits, and adjoining streets, according to the Plat Book in the

---

[11] Barker uses terms, references and quotes that reflect white America's attitudes and theories of the day, the early 1960s. For example, the "curses" mentioned in the Armes' quote are rejected by virtually all Christian theologians today, and referring to African Americans as "Negroes" was not considered demeaning at the time.

St. Louis County Recorder's office, are not to be resided on in perpetuity by anyone of [Negro] descent.

PROPOSITION

The important thing to me as a minister is not how far or fast the Negro rises, but what our *attitude* toward this situation is. How does the race issue apply to us who are Christians? To us, of all people, it should make no difference at all [what race a person bears]. According to God['s Word], any individual Negro is either our neighbor or our brother, and in either case we are to love him. *If race means something to us, it is evidence that Christ has not come to mean enough.*

1.

First, let us realize that every Negro is to be regarded as our neighbor, whom we are to love as ourselves. Paul, in Athens, was in the America of his day. Athens was that great democracy, yet Athenians also were confident of their superiority, having legendarily sprouted divinely from the soil of Attica. But Paul's message in Acts 17 was that there is only one true God, who made the world (17:26a). The word "blood" is not there, but not needed. Paul's point is a basic one. It is a statement of our whole covenant theology: that all are descended from Adam, and in Adam all die, but in Christ we can all be made alive (Acts 17:3b). The whole world is under common judgment (Rom. 3:22-23). This was directed to Jews, who were proud of their race. "There is no difference, for all have sinned…"

When we consider black people, the first thing to recognize is that before God, we are all in the same boat, and nothing else matters so much.

(a) Jack Armes, a missionary to Kenya, was recently on furlough here, and was asked why Negro peoples generally were more backward and slow in development of civilization, since anthropologists tell us that there is no basic difference between the races. Jack answered that the curse of Noah on the descendants of Ham may very well be a factor, but we have no reason to enforce it. It means that they are to be pitied rather than blamed. ...In reality, all mankind is under a curse, but God has shown us that he loves us enough for his son to die for us.[12]

(b) Jesus stressed the unity of the human race in the parable of the Good Samaritan, in which a man was robbed and beaten, but ignored by a Jew. A Levite passed by and ignored the man. A priest did the same. Then a Samaritan[13] came and helped. Jesus told this parable in answer to the question "Who is my neighbor?"—as in "Love your neighbor as yourself." The Jews despised the Samaritans. But Jesus is pointing out that when it comes to human need, there are no race distinctions. All the human race is in need, in God's sight.

Application 1: We teach children to sing "Jesus Loves the Little Children..." Yet we are prone to live a quite different example, and what are our children to think of our conversation when we speak of "niggers" in that [particular] tone of voice? We sing "I'm only a sinner saved by grace," yet act as though it makes some difference whether we are a white-skinned sinner or a black-skinned one. You who think a Negro should "keep his place," who do you think you are? (Eph. 2:12-13; 1 Cor. 6:11). It makes no sense for us to support missionary work in Kenya and

---

[12] See ftn. 11.

[13] Samaritans were despised by the Jews.

not be sensitive to the spiritual needs of Negroes here. If the Gospel means anything—and its first element is that all have sinned and need salvation—then our church doors must be open to everyone who wishes to come to Christ. Our hearts must be equally open. What do you do when canvassing the neighborhood for our church if a door were opened to your knock to reveal a dark-skinned face? Remember, his soul is no darker or lighter than the next person's, and it is to lighten his soul with the Gospel that you are there. He is your neighbor, in need.

2.

Second, the Negro can be our brother. There are only two kinds of people in God's eyes: sinners and sinners saved. And God makes it clear repeatedly that the Gospel of salvation is for all, regardless of who they are (Rom. 10:11-13).

(a) Paul was once a proud Jew. But when he was saved, he realized that all things that had meant so much [before] were of no significance, but were to be counted but dung. To him, Christ meant all. In a Jewish prayer book, we find this: "Blessed art thou, O Lord Our God, who hast not made me a heathen…a bondman…a woman." This is like the Pharisee's prayer—and Paul was a Pharisee. Yet once a Christian, he writes that no cultural, educational, economic or social distinction [is meaningful] (Gal. 3:28). Not even sex, insofar as the relationship of the individual soul to Christ is concerned. Obviously, these distinctions still exist, but they are not relevant in terms of the Gospel. The only significant thing is that I am a sinner, and Christ saved me, and here is someone else in the same experience. Nothing else is of comparable importance. Col. 3:10-11 brings out the matter of race distinction. Scythians were like gypsy warriors: filthy habits, never washing with water, drank the blood of the first enemy killed in battle, made napkins of scalps and drinking from bowls [made] of skulls. Once in Christ, though, even this sort of background was of no essential difference.

(b) It dismays me to see white pickets carrying signs claiming that the Bible teaches the separation of races. That is just not there in the Bible. It is true that the Hebrews of the Old Testament were to be distinct from other peoples because as a *nation* they were God's people. Even so, Ruth was received [into the Jewish nation], and became an ancestor of David and Christ. In New Testament times, the Ethiopian Eunuch was received [into the community of believers]. And whatever distinctions existed in the Old Testament no longer apply, except that as Christians, we are to be distinct from unbelief.

Application 2: People who are concerned about the race question stress most the danger of intermarriage. If only Christians were equally concerned about the intermarriage of believers and unbelievers! This is what God opposes. I know of Christian parents whose daughter was dating a Christian fellow who is part American Indian. Her mother was scandalized. Now that girl is married to a fine, responsible, decent white man, but with no evidence of being a real believer in Christ. I can remember my parents telling me this: It matters not what color of girl I bring to them to be my wife, as long as she is a Christian. Here is the only important difference. Is the person in Christ or out of Christ? It is the color of the heart that matters, and it is dark with sin unless washed in the blood of Christ. *If race still means something to any of us, it is evidence that Christ doesn't mean enough.*

SERMON CONCLUSION

It is said that the race problem hurts our foreign relations. No, it hurts our spiritual relations. There is no congregation of black people in the Reformed Presbyterian denomination, and only a few, to my knowledge, are integrated. Our denomination's mission in Grand Cayman Island, south of Cuba, has gone back and forth between World Presbyterian Mission and National Presbyterian Missions, partly because of the race question. Meanwhile, young people need to be trained to minister to their own people. If they come to Covenant College, and were to attend church here, what will our attitude be? May it be one honoring to Christ, who saved us, regarding the Negro as our neighbor and our brother.

That was it. Simply a sermon, given by a part-time preacher, probably to a scant summertime congregation. Nothing earth-shaking happened during or after the service. Likely, some of the Covenant College and Seminary students in attendance that day learned that they needed to improve their attitudes toward the "Negro," and not to join pickets carrying signs claiming that the Bible teaches the separation of races, but all in all, it was just a sermon. Closing hymn, benediction, exit.

But this sermon was going to "trouble the water" in the Reformed Presbyterian Church with respect to this tiny denomination's relationship with people of color. African Americans and whites were going to be invited to "wade in" together, and as John Wesley Work II (1871-1925), a black songwriter wrote, when they did so the waters would be troubled, and healing would result:[14]

---

[14] The reference is to Jesus' healing of an invalid at the Pool of Bethesda, recorded in John 5. The King James Version includes this verse: "For an angel went down at a certain season into the pool, and troubled the water: whosoever then first after the troubling of the water stepped in was made whole of whatsoever disease he had." (Jn. 5:4).

Wade in the Water[15]

Wade in the water
Wade in the water children
Wade in the water
God's gonna trouble the water

Who's that young girl[16] dressed in red
Wade in the water
Must be the children that Moses led
God's gonna trouble the water

Chorus

    Wade in the water, wade in the water children
    Wade in the water,
    God's gonna trouble the water

Who's that young girl dressed in white
Wade in the water
Must be the children of the Israelite
Oh, God's gonna trouble the water

Chorus

Who's that young girl dressed in blue
Wade in the water
Must be the children that's coming through,
God's gonna trouble the water, yeah

Chorus

The preaching of the Word is meant to trouble the water. It is intended to have real, substantial effect in the believer's life, and thus in the life of the human race. More than that, biblical

---

[15] "Wade in the Water" lyrics copyrighted BMG Rights Management US, LLC (used by permission).

[16] See mention of Peaches Ricks, p.35. Arline Cadwell recalls that Peaches walked into the first meeting of Third Street Sunday School (see ch. 3) wearing a dress, but cannot recall the color, which leaves us free to imagine red, white or blue.

preaching *does* have such effect. It does bear fruit, it sanctifies, it brings to maturity, it builds God's Church. John Calvin argues:

> Paul says that our Savior "ascended far above all heavens, that he might fill all things. And he gave some, apostles; and some, prophets; and some, evangelists; and some, pastors and teachers; for the perfecting of the saints, for the work of the ministry, for the edifying of the body of Christ: till we all come to the unity of the faith, and of the knowledge of the Son of God, unto a perfect man, unto the measure of the stature of the fullness of Christ" (Eph. 4:10-13). We see that God, who might perfect his people in a moment, chooses not to bring them to manhood in any other way than by the education of the Church. We see the mode of doing it expressed: *the preaching of celestial doctrine is committed to pastors.*[17] (emphasis added)

Will Barker was such a pastor. He didn't know what would happen as a result of his preaching this sermon. Nothing visible did happen, not for some years to follow. Just a simple exposition of Scripture. No hullabaloo; not a ribbon-cutting ceremony. God quietly plants seeds through his preachers and teachers, and even they don't know what's going to come of those seeds. Usually all of us just have to wait and see what God has in mind, meanwhile being fully assured that he *does* have something in mind:

> So shall my word be that goes out from my mouth;
> > it shall not return to me empty,
> > but it shall accomplish that which I purpose,
> > and shall succeed in the thing for which I sent it.[18]

A seed was planted that morning, and it was to bear some exciting fruit. Calvin's "celestial doctrine" had been preached. God's word would not return to him empty and would accom-

---

[17] Calvin, John, *Institutes of the Christian Religion*, ed. John T. McNeill, trans. Ford Lewis Battles. 2 vols. Louisville KY: Westminster Press, 1960, IV,i,5, p.674.

[18] Isa. 55:11.

plish that which he purposed. Nobody knew it, but New City Fellowship was on its way.

2.

WILMINGTON SYNOD (1968)

"Your word is a lamp to my feet and a light to my path."
—Psalm 119:105

ONE OF THOSE attending the June 16, 1963, worship service at Hazelwood Reformed Presbyterian Church was Rudolph Schmidt. Rudy was registrar at Covenant College and Covenant Seminary, both located on the same campus in suburban St. Louis at the time. Rudy was one of Will Barker's elders at the Hazelwood church. Collyn, Rudy's wife, was also in attendance. Collyn was dean of women at the college.

Barker's Influence on Rudy Schmidt

Rudy was not unenlightened about race issues in America. He had a master's degree in history from St. Louis University, and he taught courses in American History at Covenant College. He knew a great deal about slavery, the Civil War, Jim Crow laws, and segregation as it existed in America in the 1960s. But he would later state that prior to Will Barker's sermon, he hadn't really thought much about racial conflicts within the context of scripture. He would also say that Will's sermon transformed the way he looked at the white Christian's attitude toward African Americans.

Neither Rudy nor Collyn—nor, for that matter, Will Barker—were what one might call activists. Will was the quintessential professor: soft-spoken, kindly, demurring, nuanced. Rudy was quiet, usually listening rather than expressing opinions. Neither Will nor Rudy was impulsive or quick to state their position on any subject without thinking it through thoroughly. Yet for those who knew them well, it was obvious that they did form strong opinions, and once they formed them, they were not easily dissuaded.

Covenant College Moves South

The Barkers and the Schmidts were especially busy in 1963. In the latter part of that year Covenant College, outgrowing the St. Louis campus it shared with Covenant Seminary, purchased "The Castle in the Clouds" on top of Lookout Mountain. The college faculty and staff were occupied with preparing for the move, which took place in the summer of 1964. These two couples moved with the college, taking up residence on the mountain, which straddles the Georgia-Tennessee line and overlooks the city of Chattanooga.

Reformed Presbyterian Church of Lookout Mountain

There were no churches in the area at the time that were member congregations of the Evangelical Presbyterian Church, the denomination that owned and operated Covenant College.[19] Some of the college constituency began to worship at Lookout Mountain Presbyterian Church, First Presbyterian Church or Westminster Presbyterian Church, the latter two in downtown Chattanooga. (All three of these churches were in the Presbyterian Church in the United States, then commonly known as the

---

[19] It was at a joint meeting of the synods of the Reformed Presbyterian Church of North America and the Evangelical Presbyterian Church in April 1965, convened at Covenant College, that the two denominations merged, forming the "Reformed Presbyterian Church, Evangelical Synod" (RPCES).

Southern Presbyterian Church). But many folks at the college understandably wanted a church in their own denomination, and so one was formed in 1965: the First Reformed Presbyterian Church of Lookout Mountain. It met at the college in the beginning, and Tom Jones, a gifted preacher and graduate of Covenant Seminary, was called as pastor.

General Synod, 1966

Rudy Schmidt was one of the original elders at Lookout Mountain Reformed Presbyterian Church. Will Barker, head of the college's history department, also attended the church. It was in this capacity that both of them attended the synod meeting at Covenant College's mountaintop campus in 1965 where the RPCES was formed. At that meeting the synod appointed a committee to study "racial questions," to report back to the 1966 synod.

Charles Anderson, Bible professor at Covenant College, was appointed chair of the committee; Will Barker was on it as well. During the year, the committee met and drafted the following report, which was adopted by the 1966 General Synod:

> [T]he Bible maintains the unity of the human race before the one redeemer and judge, Jesus Christ; if the "Hamitic curse" applies at all to the Negro, it is as something to be counteracted by the Gospel; the confusing of tongues at the Tower of Babel was because of sin and in no way prevents unity for the glory of God—in fact Pentecost indicates the opposite; the Good Samaritan points us to "love thy neighbor" as the essence of the Christian life and shows that this includes the most despised member of the human race; James' admonition against respect of persons rules out any discrimination in the matter of church attendance as contrary to the faith and as sin; and genuine love for God (and genuine salvation) is revealed in a genuine love for all the brethren.

We look upon our approach to the Negro, whether Christian or unbeliever, in a spirit of repentance, and we exhort one another to greater obedience to the Great Commission commandment to His disciples of whatever race, "That ye love one another, as I have loved you, that ye also love one another" (John 13:34).[20]

The sentence, "We look upon our approach to the Negro... in a spirit of repentance," is telling. In using the word "repentance," Synod was acknowledging that the church had something to repent of. Racial discrimination was tacitly, if not expressly, acknowledged. It was being acknowledged not because blacks were taking the floor to raise the issue because there weren't any blacks on the floor to raise the issue. Synod took this action because the commissioners, or a majority of them, knew that racial discrimination existed in their small denomination and was out of accord with what the Bible taught. They declared their intent to repent and right the ship.

General Synod, 1968:
Racial Intermarriage Debate

But for some this "report on racial questions" left open for further study the issue of interracial marriage. So the committee was reconstituted in 1967 to make a further study of that volatile issue and report back to Synod. It did so at the May 1968 synod meeting in Wilmington, Delaware. The committee recommended that Synod adopt the position that Scripture in no way prohibits or disfavors interracial marriage. Will Barker was the chairman and presented the committee's report on the floor of synod.

He remembers that in the morning session, the matter was hotly debated, and by lunch break he was a bit tired of answering

---

[20] Summary, "Report of the Committee on Racial Questions," Minutes of the 144th General Synod of the RPCES, May 4, 1966. St. Louis, MO: PCA Historical Center, http://www.pcahistory.org/findingaids/rpces/ docsynod/385. html (accessed August 26, 2017), pp.51-54.

questions and arguing. Mostly, though, he was discouraged, fearing that Synod would vote against the committee's recommendation. So instead of eating, he prayed (a very brief fast). And when he returned to the meeting after lunch, everything had changed. He says it was like someone had turned on a light. Synod passed the recommendation, which reads:

> I Corinthians 6:15-16; 7:16,39. These verses relate to the subject of intermarriage, especially the last verse, and the last clause: "only in the Lord." It is striking that in all of Paul's discussion of marriage this is the one principle that is stressed in regard to whom one should marry. This is not to say that marriage to any Christian is necessarily expedient, but the only marriage clearly prohibited is that of a believer to an unbeliever. The Bible does not teach that interracial marriage of believers is morally wrong. We do recognize that children of a mixed marriage born into a prejudiced society face a serious problem of identity. This problem of identity is largely overcome, however, where the commitment to Christ is uppermost, and where the church welcomes all who are in covenant relationship to the Lord into its fellowship. Although marriage between the races should be approached with caution because of the serious nature of the difficulties involved, nevertheless we are persuaded that God's blessing is promised to all who marry *in the Lord*.[21] (emphasis added)

It was no accident that this report began with a Scripture reference. The compact argument presented in the report was little more than an exposition of Scripture. No mention was made of the Declaration of Independence (that "all men are created equal"), of social studies, of human moral codes, of current trends. In the wider public arena, all of those things and count-

---

[21] "Report of the Committee on Racial Questions," Minutes of the 146th General Synod, May 14, 1968. St. Louis, MO: PCA Historical Center, http://www.pcahistory.org/findingaids/rpces/docsynod/388.html: 25-27 (accessed August 26, 2017).

less more could appropriately have been cited as authority. But the committee, and the synod commissioners, wanted to be on absolutely safe ground. Thankfully, the only thing that carried weight in the court of this church was the Word of God. These men were faithful to their oath taken at ordination:[22] *sola scriptura*. If those commissioners had voted on the basis of their personal feelings, preferences and prejudices that day, the result could easily have been the reverse. The church today can be thankful that vows mattered to these men.

Revivals in ancient Israel were always preceded by a "fresh look" at the written Word. For example, in the revival that came soon after young King Josiah took the throne,[23] a copy of Moses' law was found in the temple. Apparently it had been discarded but looked kind of important to Hilkiah, the high priest who found it. Hilkiah had it couriered to the king, and Josiah had somebody read it to him; he then had it read to all the priests and the people of Israel. The Israelites repented, and changed their ways. A great revival followed; God once again brought blessing on his people.

Immediate Reaction to 1968 Synod Action on Interracial Marriage

In our case, in the 20th century, who would have thought that a vote on the subject of interracial marriage, taken in an all-white denomination, would have any significant impact? You might think that it would just be printed up in the minutes and lie buried in the archives—maybe an interesting historical note, but little more. Instead it had an impact even before the minutes of the meeting were published. It took less than three weeks.

---

[22] Question 2 of the *Westminster Shorter Catechism* is: "What rule hath God given to direct us how we may glorify and enjoy him?" and the answer reads: "The Word of God, which is contained in the Scriptures of the Old and New Testaments, is the only rule to direct us how we may glorify and enjoy him" (i.e., *sola scriptura*).

[23] Recorded in the parallel passages of 2 Ki. 22-23 and 2 Chron. 34-35.

After the vote, Will Barker, Rudy and Collyn Schmidt and another elder from Lookout Mountain RPC, Charles Donaldson, traveled the 700 miles back from Wilmington to Chattanooga in the same car. Will remembers that Rudy was quiet for the first part of the trip. Apparently he was mulling things over, as he was prone to do.

Finally, he spoke up: "Well, now that we've voted on it, it's time for us to *do* something about it." And he did.

Synod had ended on May 17. As soon as Rudy and Collyn got back to their home on Lookout Mountain, they began to make phone calls, recruiting and organizing folks from Covenant College to canvass one of the many blighted areas of Chattanooga, this one near the intersection of East Third and Cherry Streets. They wanted to start a Sunday school in the neighborhood.

They contacted a Christian woman from Lookout Mountain, Collette Grady, now a member of their church. She had inherited some run-down apartment buildings on Third Street from her recently-deceased lawyer husband. From her they secured a two-bedroom apartment so they would have a place to meet. They mimeographed fliers for the canvassers to distribute, inviting people who lived in the area to join them for a new Sunday school, which was to meet just 16 days after the synod vote.

So "Third Street Sunday School" was scheduled to have its first meeting on the morning of June 2, 1968. New City Fellowship was about to be born. God was honoring a greater church that was, by his grace, serious about being faithful to his Word, "to walk after the Lord and to keep his commandments and his testimonies and his statutes" (1 Ki. 23:3b).

32 · EVERY PRECIOUS STONE

3.

THIRD STREET SUNDAY SCHOOL

"Do not despise these small beginnings, for the Lord rejoices to see the work begin."—ZECHARIAH 4:10A (NLT)

D R. MARTIN LUTHER KING, JR. may have spoken prophetically about what was about to happen at Third Street and Cherry in Chattanooga in his famous *I Have a Dream* speech in 1963:

> And I say to you today my friends, let freedom ring. From the prodigious hilltops of New Hampshire, let freedom ring. From the mighty mountains of New York, let freedom ring. From the mighty Alleghenies of Pennsylvania! Let freedom ring from the snow-capped Rockies of Colorado! Let freedom ring from the curvaceous slopes of California! But not only there; let freedom ring from the Stone Mountain of Georgia! Let freedom ring from Lookout Mountain in Tennessee![24]

LOOKOUT MOUNTAIN

King's address was on August 28, 1963. Two months later, on October 26, the trustees of Covenant College in St. Louis were notified by one of its board members that a former luxury

---

[24] Excerpt of transcript of speech by Dr. Martin Luther King Jr., August 28, 1963. https://www.archives.gov/files/press/exhibits/dream-speech.pdf (accessed September 23, 2018).

hotel atop Lookout Mountain, "The Castle in the Clouds," was up for sale. On November 30 the board voted to purchase it for $250,000, and the school moved there in 1964.[25] The purchase was made exactly 100 years after the Civil War Battle of Lookout Mountain which was fought at the end of November 1863. In that battle Union troops took the mountain, helping to break a stranglehold the Confederacy had on the city of Chattanooga.[26]

In 1963 the Covenant College board could not have envisioned that some of their own faculty would, five years later, start a little Sunday School at the foot of that lofty mountain—a mission that would mature into New City Fellowship. Dr. King was assassinated on April 4 1968; Third Street Sunday School began two months later. Though King was gone, God was honoring his hopes and vision. A new freedom was about to ring out from Lookout Mountain.

Into the Fray

Arline Wetzel (now Cadwell) was a close friend of Collyn Schmidt in those days. Both worked at Covenant College, both were members of Lookout Mountain Reformed Presbyterian Church, and both had a new-found and vigorous interest in outreach to the poor and racial reconciliation. Both had also come down from Lookout Mountain into the streets of Chattanooga to prepare for the startup of a new Sunday school. For two weeks prior to its first meeting, they and others they had recruited canvassed the neighborhood, pounding the hot pavement, handing out mimeographed invitations, welcoming anyone who would listen to come to the new Sunday School.

So of course Arline was in attendance when it met for the first time on June 2, 1968, in an apartment provided by Collette Grady, a Christian woman from Lookout Mountain who had in-

---

[25] See p.26.

[26] Eicher, David J., *The Longest Night: A Military History of the Civil War*. New York: Simon & Schuster (2001), p.610.

herited the apartment complex from her lawyer husband. Arline recalls:

> We arrived in the apartment that morning, ready to sing and teach, not knowing what to expect, or if any children would attend.
>
> A few minutes after we planned to start, just as we began to wonder if anyone would come, the Lord brought us a little girl named Peaches Ricks, who entered the apartment. Soon, other children began to appear, until a [total of 15] children arrived that morning.
>
> They all took their places as we sang our first song together, "Fairest Lord Jesus," which Rudy [Schmidt] had carefully printed on a flip chart that he held up. After opening exercises, the children were divided into age-appropriate classes and went to their "classrooms": a class in each of the two bedrooms, one in the kitchen, one in the living room, and maybe one in the dining room.[27]

Prophetic Vision

Makeshift, pretty much experimental, and *small*. No hymnals, no overhead projector, so someone has to use a "flip chart" in order to guide the children through "Fairest Lord Jesus." But what a great song for the children to sing. Its last stanza is:

> Beautiful Savior! Lord of all the nations!
> Son of God and Son of Man!
> Glory and honor, praise, adoration,
> Now and forevermore be Thine.

Fifteen kids and a few adults singing prophetically, *Lord of all the nations!*

New City Fellowship St. Louis has for many years described itself on the web as, "WHERE THE NATIONS COME TOGETHER TO WORSHIP JESUS," and the mix of ethnic groups becomes im-

---

[27] Cadwell, Arline, "History of New City Fellowship" (undated), p.2.

mediately evident to any visitor to its worship services. Such was in microcosm on June 2, 1968, in that little apartment on East Third Street. It was almost all children, but Jesus asked, "Have you never read, 'From the lips of children and infants you, Lord, have called forth your praise'?"[28]

Holy Spirit Present

The story is told of an African-American fellow traveling by train many years ago through a southern city, where he had a layover. He got into the station about 8:00 on a Sunday morning, and his connecting train didn't depart until the afternoon. He wanted to attend a worship service and found a church a few blocks from the station. He went up to the front door where a deacon met him and told him that people of his color weren't permitted. Undaunted, he went to the side door, the opposite side door, then to the back. He got the same answer at all four doors. He gave up, walked back toward the train station and prayed aloud, "O Lord, you know I really wanted to attend church today, but they wouldn't let me in. You know my heart, so please forgive me." A voice came from heaven: "Don't worry about it, son. For years I've been trying to get into that place myself."

Maybe the Lord wasn't welcome at that particular church building on that Sunday morning, but he was welcome at Third Street Sunday School for their first worship service. Jesus made that fact crystal clear.

The St. Louis NCF congregation often sings the Benny Hinn song, "Holy Spirit, Thou Art Welcome in This Place." Jesus said, "Whoever welcomes one of these little children in my name welcomes me; and whoever welcomes me does not welcome me but the one who sent me."[29] When Collyn Schmidt and Arline Wet-

---

[28] Mt. 21:16b (NIV). Jesus was citing David: "Through the praise of children and infants you have established a stronghold against your enemies, to silence the foe and the avenger." (Psa. 8:2, NIV).

[29] Mk. 9:37 (NIV).

zel walked about the back streets of Chattanooga inviting little children to a new Sunday school, and when they opened the door on Sunday morning and welcomed little Peaches Ricks across the threshold, they were actually welcoming the Holy Spirit into the apartment. He walked in with Peaches.

The Day of Small Things

During the summer following that first meeting Arline and the Schmidts, now joined by Covenant College students Steve Kaufmann, Mary Belz and others from Covenant, continued to beat the pavement, inviting children to come, sometimes walking children to the apartment on Sunday mornings. These volunteers assisted in teaching the children as well, and, when Sunday school was over, they would drive back up the mountain to attend their regular church services.

Third Street Sunday School was comprised almost entirely of children, and it remained that way for some time. Arline further recalls:

> After our first day of classes, we continued in that small apartment for almost four more years, adding many more children and two adult women.
>
> Aunt Collyn [Schmidt] met with those two ladies in the kitchen—one or two more might have exceeded its capacity. I met with my class of girls in a bedroom, but as our numbers grew, my class 'graduated' to the hallway.
>
> The apartment in which we were meeting had probably been very modern when it was first built but when we were there, it was a bit archaic. It had a small room with just a toilet, and another room with a sink and a tub. After meeting in that hallway, our class then graduated again to the "tub" room. It had a claw-foot bathtub with space all around it, so the girls sat around the edge of the inside of the tub with their feet on the bottom, and I sat

on one end, teaching the lesson. I'm sorry I don't have any pictures to prove it!

That was about as strange as when I taught my class for many weeks in my car: the girls sat crowded in the front and back seats, and I sat on my knees with my back against the door and the steering wheel. The Lord gave my Sunday School class patience and the ability to be flexible.[30]

Many of us today, enjoying the comfort of air-conditioned sanctuaries and padded pews, often worshiping with hundreds of others, would do well to remember the humble beginnings of Third Street Sunday School. The "patience" and "ability to be flexible" of five or six little African-American children sitting on the edge of a bathtub or packed together into the backseat of a car—those little things have made the church the beneficiary of something great. We should never despise "the day of small things" in the church. Someday, the prophet Zechariah writes, the small things, the humble and often despised things, those feeble efforts that may have seemed insignificant at the time, will cause us to rejoice (Zech. 4:10).[31]

---

[30] Cadwell, pp.3-4.

[31] "[Jesus] told them another parable: 'The kingdom of heaven is like a mustard seed, which a man took and planted in his field. Though it is the smallest of all seeds, yet when it grows, it is the largest of garden plants and becomes a tree, so that the birds come and perch in its branches.' " (Mt. 13:31-32). Similarly, the Apostle Paul wrote that "God chose what is foolish in the world to shame the wise; God chose what is weak in the world to shame the strong; God chose what is low and despised in the world, even things that are not, to bring to nothing things that are." (1 Cor. 1:27-28).

4.

RANDY & JOAN

"And he called the twelve and began to send them out two by two."
—Mark 6:7 (niv)

THEY CAME TO US from the Newark, New Jersey "projects," some of the most poverty-stricken government housing in the United States during the 1950s and '60s. That's where they grew up, where they met, fell in love and eventually married. She was black; he was white; both were poor. The grinding poverty they experienced wasn't voluntary, and it wasn't their fault. But it was their life.

They didn't know it at the time, but Joan McRae and Randy Nabors were being prepared by God for a life calling. They were learning first-hand what it means to be poor, to be dependent on others, to be constantly in need. They were learning that poverty is brutal, and brings shame. They were learning, as Randy has written, that poverty is "insulting."[32] They were learning what poor people go through, what they felt like, what their outlook on life was, because they *were* those poor people.

---

[32] Nabors, Randy, *Merciful: The Opportunity and Challenge of Discipling the Poor Out of Poverty* (Preface), Kindle Edition (2015), location 168.

Responses to Poverty

There are many ways that they might have responded to their poverty. They could have tried to accept it, to tell themselves that this is just their lot in life. Or they might have become bitter, blaming society, government, or even God, for their plight. Or they might have been tempted by the "Reader's Digest" kind of story about poor people who, by sheer wit, pluck, luck, and hard work, pulled themselves up by the bootstraps, becoming CEOs of billion-dollar corporations, famous football players, world-renowned surgeons. They learned that for the most part that is a myth. Rather than being encouraging, it can easily plunge a poor person into a deeper despair, because the fact is that try as they might, most simply cannot get out of the fix they're in without help.

And yet each of these responses has a bit of truth mixed in. Accepting poverty as one's "station" in life could possibly be justified on the basis of scripture: "Keep your life free from love of money, and be content with what you have…"[33] Becoming bitter because of poverty is at least understandable when those claiming to be Christians say, "God bless you! Keep warm and eat well!" but they don't share with you the necessities of life.[34] And there's nothing wrong with trying to extricate yourself from poverty by willpower and diligence because after all, "those who work hard will prosper."[35] Even then, some work hard at menial jobs or even not-so-menial ones and don't exactly prosper.

Mercy

But Randy and Joan learned something in their poverty that "none of the above" has to offer. They learned by experience that

---

[33] Heb. 13:5a.
[34] James 2:15-16.
[35] Prov. 13:4b.

God, typically through his servants, is merciful. They learned what it meant for Christians to "love on" them, to help them, to provide for them when they didn't have enough groceries to keep hunger away. They learned that the gospel could be communicated powerfully through simple acts of mercy in the name of Jesus. Randy, in his book *Merciful: The Opportunity and Challenge of Discipling the Poor Out of Poverty*, recalls this from his childhood in Newark:

> Probably the greatest impression on me occurred one day when I realized my mother was weeping, seated at the kitchen table. We'd run out of food and there was nothing to eat... [My mom was] crying at the table, unable to figure out where to get food. But I remember hearing a knock at our door. My sisters and I ran to open the door, and there were the deacons of Calvary Gospel Church, holding bags of groceries for us.[36]

Growing up destitute produces something more than head knowledge about poverty. Poverty registers in the gut. Randy *felt* poverty. But just as surely, when his own mom was crying because she couldn't put food on the table, opening the door to people who were lugging bags of groceries produced something more than head knowledge about mercy. Mercy registers in the gut too. He *felt* mercy. He *felt* what it's like to be loved, valued and cared for, and it has deeply affected his ministry to others ever since.

Calvary Gospel Church

It was through the outreach ministry of Calvary Gospel Church in Newark that Randy, age 9, became a Christian. His mother, a single mom, had been attending a women's Bible study and was invited to attend an evangelistic service at the church.

---

[36] *Merciful*, p.12.

She went. Kennedy Smartt[37] was the visiting evangelist, and he believed in follow-up. It was his policy to visit new attendees as soon as possible after an evangelistic service. So Kennedy Smartt and the pastor of Calvary Gospel Church, Grover Willcox, were there knocking at the Nabors' door the next morning. Randy's mom invited them in, they talked, presented the gospel, and prayed with mother and children as they all sat around the kitchen table. A great transaction occurred that morning in the heart of Newark: Gloria Nabors and her children chose to follow Christ. The whole family crossed over from death to life.[38]

It was at Calvary Gospel that Randy got his first glimpse of pretty Joan McRae, and when he did, he told himself that this was the girl he was going to marry. Joan had begun to attend the church and get involved with the youth group. Greatly influenced by the pastor, Grover Willcox, as well as her two Christian "church-lady" grandmothers, Joan became a Christian at age 15. Pastor Willcox asked Randy to walk Joan home to her apartment one time after youth group. Randy could hardly believe this stroke of good luck, and the rest is history.

Pursuit of Joan

Calvary Gospel Church had a connection with Peniel Bible Camp at Lake Luzerne in upstate New York. For kids otherwise

---

[37] Kennedy Smartt, preacher-evangelist, would later become a founding father of the Presbyterian Church in America (see p.157). Dr. Smartt is credited with planting the seeds for what became "Evangelism Explosion" in 1962 under the leadership of the late D. James Kennedy. Jim Kennedy, whose Ft. Lauderdale FL church had fallen to just 17 members, received an invitation from Smartt to assist in evangelistic services in Scottdale GA. During the 10 days of meetings, Kennedy went out with Smartt and "...watched him engage people spiritually. By the end of the meetings, 54 people made professions of faith in Christ. [Jim Kennedy] returned to Fort Lauderdale with the seeds that eventually became Evangelism Explosion. His church began to grow, and grow. In a brief 12-year period, church membership increased from 17 to 2,000." *Evangelism Explosion: History,* https://evangelismexplosion.org/about-us/history/ (accessed July 31, 2018).

[38] *Merciful,* p.10. See Jn. 5:24.

imprisoned by the hot bricks and concrete of the Newark projects during the summer months, it was just what the doctor ordered. Calvary's youth group made it possible for every teenager to attend during summer vacation. Joan was one of those who went to Peniel in the summer of 1967, following her graduation from high school in Newark.

Pastor Willcox made no secret of his desire for every one of the young people in his congregation to go to a Christian college. He gave Joan application forms to complete for various colleges. Joan didn't want to disappoint her pastor, and so she was compliant enough to fill them out, but she then literally "shelved" the applications because she wasn't considering college at all—Christian or otherwise. She assumed that she would just forgo higher education and try to get a job like her Newark high school classmates.

At Peniel, a recruiter from Covenant College, Bryant Black, was scheduled to speak on the importance of Christian education at the college level. Joan intentionally skipped his talk, knowing it would be about why high school grads should go to a Christian college, blah blah blah. She went to Peniel's swimming pool instead for a sunbathing session. Not interested. But Grover Willcox noticed that she wasn't there when Black spoke, and so he and Black together tracked her down at the swimming pool. Both stood there, poolside, to be sure that she would complete the application to Covenant and sign it. Then, because Willcox had figured out that Joan had a penchant for not mailing such papers, Black took it from her hand, stuffed it into his briefcase, and delivered it in person to the Office of Admissions, Covenant College, Lookout Mountain, Georgia 30750. Pack your bags, Joan! You're on your way to Covenant!

Both Randy and Joan were *pursued*. Grover Willcox and Kennedy Smartt believed that they had more work to do after the benediction following the evangelistic preaching service; they pursued the Nabors family the next morning by going to Gloria

Nabors' apartment in the Projects. Bryant Black didn't think his job was over either when he had finished his recruitment talk at Peniel; he, with Grover Willcox, pursued resistant Joan McRae at the swimming pool. All three of these men were intentional, determined, and persistent. And their doggedness has borne fruit.

Covenant College

That poolside summit was in July 1967, and by the end of August Joan was at Covenant, high atop Lookout Mountain. She had no money, but with a loan and a work-study scholarship she could make it through at least the first year. And she could sing, *really* sing. She joined the Covenant College Chorale. Randy, still in Newark, went to hear them when the chorale visited the New York area. Joan, of course, was his main interest, but Randy reports being "blown away" when he heard the chorale close with the college hymn, "All for Jesus":

> All for Jesus, all for Jesus!
> All my being's ransomed pow'rs:
> All my thoughts and words and doings,
> All my days and all my hours.[39]

Surely part of the reason Randy felt "blown away" by this hymn was that the girl he loved was in the choir. But the words resonated with him: "All for Jesus; all my days and all my hours." That was exactly where Joan the singer and Randy the adoring listener were. Whatever it meant—and in 1967 they knew very little of what it would mean for them—they had been brought to that point in their lives.

Randy came to Covenant too, but not immediately. A friend at Calvary Gospel Church, interested in seeing Randy go to a Christian college, paid his way to Biola College (originally the Bible Institute of Los Angeles, now Biola University). Randy en-

---

[39] "All for Jesus," stanza 1, Mary D. James (1871). Dr. Robert G. Rayburn, first president of Covenant College, chose this as the college hymn when the college began in Pasadena, California in 1955.

rolled there for the 1968-69 school year, meanwhile continuing what was now a long-distance romance with Joan. It was good education, and during that time he did get involved with some inner-city work in the Los Angeles area. But the next school year he transferred to Covenant, the main reason being that he missed his best friends from Calvary Gospel Church, all of whom were now students on the mountain. Those friends included Rodney Alexander, Rodney Ailes, Oliver Trimiew, Patricia Riley, and most of all, as far as Randy was concerned, Joan. This Newark quintet was entirely African-American.

Third Street Sunday School

If friends mean "home," Randy came home in the fall of 1969. And Chattanooga has been his and Joan's home ever since. The two weren't married yet; that would happen the day after New Year's Day in 1971. But Joan was fully involved by this time in the just-more-than-a-year-old Third Street Sunday School, the mission work sponsored by the Reformed Presbyterian Church of Lookout Mountain. Randy naturally followed her into that work. While tending to his studies on the mountain, Randy immersed himself in this outreach ministry to the poor, especially African Americans, in the impoverished center of Chattanooga.

Rudy Schmidt was the "elder-in-charge" of the mission. During the first semester of Randy's involvement, Randy asked Rudy for permission to start up a youth ministry. Randy remembers that, "He asked me to write up a proposal. Although I never got to the proposal, I did get to the work."[40]

That says much about the relationship of these two men for years to follow, right up until Rudy's death at age 79 in 2005.[41] For all that time, Rudy was the senior ruling elder at NCF Chattanooga. He was old enough to be Randy's father, and sometimes a fatherly oversight did become evident, but on the whole this unlikely duo treated one another as peers. Randy was the ideal-

---

[40] *Merciful*, p.32.
[41] See p.71.

ist, spender and warrior; Rudy the realist, bookkeeper and worrier. And while those differences sometimes created tension, it proved to be a healthy tension resulting in a deep mutual respect. It worked because both men were first committed to Christ and the building of his kingdom. Everything else was a distant second.

Randy spent his first full summer in Chattanooga in 1970. He remembers it as "incredible." He moved from his Covenant College dorm room into the apartment downtown being used by Third Street Sunday School, in an effort to connect with Chattanooga youth. Pick-up basketball, pool halls, swimming—those and any other places or events where kids could be found—were the venues of choice. Nick Barker, Will Barker's brother and chair of the English Department at Covenant College, often accompanied Randy. They were soon joined by Rodney Alexander.

Randy and Rodney shared everything that summer—including Randy's token stipend from Reformed Presbyterian Church of Lookout Mountain. Rodney slept on the mattress, Randy on the springs. Rodney and Randy often found themselves up into the wee hours, shooting pool with neighborhood kids. By the end of that summer, they had assembled dozens of teenagers into their troupe,[42] and they all celebrated by going to Cedline Bible Camp in Spring City, Tennessee, one hour north of Chattanooga on Watts Bar Lake.

Marriage

That was Randy's last summer as a free man, and of splitting a salary with Rodney. From now on, he'd be splitting his salary and everything else with someone else. After the fall semester, as he and Joan continued to keep up with classes on the mountain and work with kids in the city, the two were married. It happened back home in Newark, during holiday break, on January 2, 1971. Lots of Chattanooga folk braved the winter cold to drive

---

[42] *Merciful*, p.35.

the 800 miles to attend, including Will Barker, by then professor of history and dean of faculty at Covenant, and his brother Nick, professor of English. Will and his wife Gail, and Nick and Sandy Barker, were at that time regulars at Third Street Sunday School. Grover Willcox, Elward Ellis and Will officiated at the wedding. (Joan and Randy now have four grown children: Michael, Garrett, Gyven, and Keren).

Early Preaching

Preaching at Third Street had begun during the fall of 1970, a duty shared by Randy and Will Barker. This was another unlikely twosome. Will, with degrees from Princeton, Cornell, Covenant Seminary and Vanderbilt, was a full professor at Covenant College, and ordained in the Reformed Presbyterian Church. All that Randy had by this time was a diploma from a Newark high school. Yet, under the guidance and authority of the Lookout Mountain RPC Session, the two began to alternate preaching duties, switching every six weeks.

This continued until Randy's graduation from Covenant in May 1972. He stayed on as the main, yet unordained, preacher for the next year. The arrangement was sanctioned by the RPC session on the mountain, even though Randy remembers that at this time he wasn't exactly "presbyterian." At the same time, he was greatly attracted to the principle of accountability in the presbyterian form of government; he sensed strongly his need of just that.

Covenant Seminary

Randy did know that if he was called to the preaching and pastoral ministry, of which he and Joan were almost certain, he needed seminary. So one day in the summer of '73 he trotted into the Covenant College Registrar's office, asking that his transcript be sent off to a seminary where he wanted to apply. "Yes," the registrar answered, "and what seminary?"

"Harvard!" Randy exclaimed.

Of course registrars have a professional and legal duty to send transcripts out to "whomever," upon nothing more than the request of a graduate. But that doesn't mean the matter can't be discussed while the transcript is being copied. That can depend on the registrar, and in this case, unfortunately for Randy, the registrar was Rudy Schmidt, who doubled as one of Randy's ruling elders.

Rudy knew how liberal and unorthodox Harvard Divinity School had become. Not, in his judgment, a good choice for learning theology. But he didn't enter into an extended debate with Randy; he just got out his Bible and read the first Psalm aloud:

> How blessed is the man who does not walk in the counsel of the wicked,
> Nor stand in the path of sinners,
> Nor sit in the seat of scoffers!
> But his delight is in the law of the Lord, and…

Rudy proceeded to read the rest of the Psalm. But he didn't really need to because Randy realized after he heard the word "scoffers" that he wasn't headed to Harvard. It really wasn't fair the way Rudy handled it: he happened to know how vulnerable Randy was when it came to scripture.

So Randy applied to Covenant Seminary, encouraged by Rudy, Robert Rayburn (then president of the seminary) and an African-American ruling elder from Augusta, Georgia, Don Sherow, who also planned to enter Covenant Seminary that fall. And Randy was also encouraged in a substantial way: a pledge from Hugh McClellan, an elder at Lookout Mountain Presbyterian Church,[43]

---

[43] Lookout Mountain Presbyterian Church, in the summer of 1973, was a member congregation of the Presbyterian Church in the United States. It later came into the Presbyterian Church in America, which was formed in December, 1973.

who promised to pay his tuition. Randy and Joan moved to Missouri in time for fall semester, 1973.

The years at Covenant College on Lookout Mountain now proved to have been but a brief respite from difficult living conditions, because once in St. Louis Randy and Joan settled into an apartment in Wellston, at the time probably the most economically depressed community in the area. And while tuition wasn't going to be a burden, they had no money to live on. True, back in Newark, where growing up was hand-to-mouth subsistence living, they had learned how to get along this way and were prepared.

But the three years of seminary were tough, and both looked forward to Randy's graduation and—hopefully—a salary paid by the government, because it was Randy's plan to enter the chaplaincy. It did seem like a more welcoming path for yet another reason: Randy and Joan weren't convinced that they'd be accepted as an interracial couple in the Reformed Presbyterian Church, whereas that would be no problem in the Army.

Call to Chattanooga

Once again, though, the pesky elders from Lookout Mountain interfered. Not long before Randy's graduation from seminary in May 1976, Rudy Schmidt and Ed Kellogg, who would later constitute the first session at NCF Chattanooga, traveled to St. Louis to visit Randy and Joan. They came armed with what was truly a Macedonian call:[44] "Come to Chattanooga and help us!"

But Randy was geared up for the chaplaincy. He told his suitors that he had filed his application for active duty already, and that he could consider their request only if his application was rejected by the Pentagon.

Well, the application wasn't rejected outright, but somehow it got lost. Oddly, Randy never heard from the Army regarding

---

[44] See Acts 16:9.

active duty.[45] He and Joan needed to make plans, and they decided to take the military's strange silence as providential. They accepted the call to Chattanooga. In July 1976, just two months after graduation from Covenant, Randy traveled to Colorado Springs, Colorado, and was ordained as a teaching elder into the Southern Presbytery of the Reformed Presbyterian Church, Evangelical Synod. He was now NCF Chattanooga's pastor. Officially.[46]

So now it was the pastorate, full time and all-out. Randy was installed as pastor of NCF Chattanooga in November 1976, at which service the Southern Presbytery also designated NCF as a "particular" church, meaning that it was on its own, no longer a mission church of Lookout Mountain RPC. His ministry as senior pastor continued until his retirement from that position in 2010—forty-four solid years of ministry, during which time the church flourished.

Kenya

There were a few breaks here and there. Randy and Joan have always had a heart for the mission field and after about five years into the NCF pastorate, developed a strong relationship with World Presbyterian Mission's[47] work in Nairobi, Kenya. Veteran missionary Sanders ("Sandy") Campbell was retiring, and Nairobi needed help. Randy and Joan decided it was time to answer that call. Randy submitted his resignation to the NCF session, by then composed of Rudy Schmidt, Ed Kellogg and Randy. He handed the letter to Rudy at a meeting where Rudy read it, then

---

[45] Randy had already been sworn in as a chaplain in 1975 and had completed chaplaincy training school by the summer of 1976. Later, after settling into the pastorate, he applied for an Army Reserve position and was called up to active duty several times after that, including during Desert Storm in 1990.

[46] One might wonder why the Southern Presbytery included both Chattanooga TN and Colorado Springs CO, 1,300 miles distant. The answer is that the RPCES was very, very small in 1976, meaning that its presbyteries were very, very spacious and its churches very far apart.

[47] World Presbyterian Mission was the foreign missions agency of the Reformed Presbyterian Church, Evangelical Synod.

looked up at Randy and said, "No." Just like that. Not an option. Ed Kellogg agreed with Rudy, and so Randy was outvoted.

Of course, no one could dictate to Randy and Joan what they could or couldn't do with their lives, but Randy rightly chose to hear the "No" vote as an affirmation of the deep affection that these men had for him, their godly counsel, and their best judgment regarding the future welfare of New City Fellowship. He and Joan yielded,[48] accepting the session's counsel. Together, however, they worked out an arrangement so that Randy and Joan could take a two-year leave of absence and help out at the Nairobi mission. They served in Africa from 1982-84 where Randy assumed the duties of pastor of Community Presbyterian Church in Nairobi. During that time, Carl Ellis, an African American, filled the NCF pulpit. Providentially, just when Randy and Joan returned to Chattanooga in 1984, Carl had received a call to a similar ministry in Baltimore, Maryland.

NCF Chattanooga Pastorate: 26 Years

From 1984 on, Randy continued uninterrupted as NCF Chattanooga's senior pastor, but in 2010 Randy and Joan decided the time had come for him to step down, or rather step aside. This time it was the session who caved, and let him do it, except that the move wasn't at all in the direction of sitting-on-the-porch retirement. Randy had by this time become Mission to North America's[49] Coordinator of Urban and Mercy Ministries. In this

---

[48] The attitude evidenced by Randy and Joan in this event is consonant with Paul's advice to the Philippians: "So if there is any encouragement in Christ, any comfort from love, any participation in the Spirit, any affection and sympathy, complete my joy by being of the same mind, having the same love, being in full accord and of one mind. Do nothing from selfish ambition or conceit, but in humility count others more significant than yourselves. Let each of you look not only to his own interests, but also to the interests of others." (Phil. 2:1-4).

[49] Mission to North America is an agency of the Presbyterian Church in America, serving PCA presbyteries and individual churches "to grow and multiply biblically healthy churches." (https://pcamna.org/wp-content/

connection, he has also become the Coordinator of New City Network, discussed in chapter 9. As of this writing, Randy Nabors is 68 years old, and still over-employed. You just can't keep a good man down.

uploads/2017/06/MNA-Brochure-May-2017.pdf) (accessed August 23, 2017).

5.

NEW CITY FELLOWSHIP, CHATTANOOGA

"But seek the welfare of the city where I have sent you into exile, and pray to the Lord on its behalf, for in its welfare you will find your welfare."—JEREMIAH 29:7.

THE ORIGINAL: it had no predecessor. The people who built it had nothing to go by—no known pattern, program or strategy. It didn't happen overnight. It wasn't really a "dream come true" either, because there wasn't a specific "dream," or blueprint, for the church in 1968; there was no plan carefully adhered to until the structure was finished. Indeed, it isn't finished yet. Though it has become a model for other ministries to build the same kind of church, ministry and outreach, it is still a work in progress.

The Vision

But from the very start of Third Street Sunday School, there was a direction. Generally, of course, it was to be biblical, and faithful to Christ in the building of his church on earth, just like any other congregation within the Body of Christ. It had moorings, anchored in Scripture. But within those broad parameters, it was also to build this particular church with particular goals,

goals that were not much evident in the traditional church at the time. Two of those goals were outreach to the poor and racial reconciliation.

The specific manner in which it was to be built, the particular ministries envisioned—those may have been a bit blurry, even unknown at the start. But those who initiated Third Street Sunday School, still attending their own Sunday school class atop Lookout Mountain, did recognize a need:

> [T]hey could not help but notice the growing city at the foot of Lookout Mountain—Chattanooga, Tennessee. They also began to notice events in society at large—the cause of civil rights and integration, the needs of the poor, and riots in the cities. They also felt a zeal to reach these people for Christ and for their denomination, which was almost exclusively white.[50]

Tom Skinner's Influence

But where to start? Of course, Third Street Sunday School was already "up and running," but the sponsors from Lookout Mountain RPC recognized that they needed to do much more than evangelize the children of a poor urban area. They began to read a book by an African-American evangelist, Tom Skinner, entitled *Black & Free*. From their study, these mostly white believers learned some indispensable principles regarding how they should exercise their zeal to reach the inner city of Chattanooga:

> The thing the white evangelical Christian must do if he wants to reach black people with the Gospel of Jesus Christ is to convince them that he considers them to be a part of society.
>
> I remember how bitter I used to get before my conversion recalling the fact that the most segregated hour of the week is eleven o'clock on Sunday morning. Before I

---

[50] Ward, Beth (editor), *New City Fellowship—Brief History* (2010), p.1.

came to Christ, the Black Nationalists showed me that the most prejudiced group of people in America are in Bible-believing, white evangelical churches. For a long time, these churches made it sound as if the only way you could get to heaven was to be white, Anglo-Saxon, Protestant, middle class and Republican!

Black people will never respond to a white person presenting the Gospel unless it is shown that black people are a part of society; that [they are] not inferior; that Christ not only died for them, too, but wants them to have the same hopes, goals, aspirations and fulfillment in life. They need to know that they can have the same social, economic, psychological, spiritual and physical opportunity as their white contemporary.[51]

This and much more comprised what one might term Skinner's "theology of racial reconciliation," and could be learned in a class more easily than it could be put into practice. The real classroom would be out on Chattanooga's streets—a sort of *practicum*.

First Worship

Actual worship services had already begun at Third Street Sunday School in January 1971, about two and a half years after its first meeting. Randy Nabors and Will Barker took alternating six-week segments of preaching. Each was well accepted—Randy the "street preacher," so far without much education (just halfway through college) and still more than five years to the end of seminary and ordination. Will had finished his Ph.D. and been ordained for eleven years. No matter; they worked well together and preached the same gospel. They also both coordinated with

---

[51] Skinner, Tom, *Black & Free* (E-book Edition) (Kindle Locations 2134-2144). Skinner Leadership Institute. Kindle Edition. Skinner's observations and principles of ministry in these areas are echoed in Randy Nabors' 1974 position paper, "Is an Integrated Church Possible?" (see Appendix 2).

Tom Skinner's counsel: respect and treat every individual, young or old, black or white, as equals.

WORSHIP STYLE AND MUSIC

Randy, Will and the other leaders at Third Street recognized early on that if their church was to show genuine respect for a different culture, worship style and music had to be different from the traditional white church. It had to be different from up on the mountain, as wonderful as that was, where singing was almost exclusively out of the "blue" Trinity Hymnal.[52] For White Anglo Saxon Protestants, this shift would prove to be quite an adventure: entering a powerful new world of music inspired by black culture. For many African Americans, it would mean learning to appreciate a more formal genre of music, the kind actually printed out with notes on the staff for soprano, alto, tenor and bass. For many whites, it meant learning to sway and clap to rhythm and maybe raise hands in worship. Those leading worship, the instrumentalists, and the music all needed to be reworked:

> Since the beginning of the Sunday School, Mrs. Collyn Schmidt had been playing a small Hammond children's organ to accompany the singing. James Ward was a Covenant College music student who put together a group to sing Edwin Hawkins style choir music. Once the worship services began to be held, he and his fiancée Beth Moore attended. He was asked if he would be willing to play for the worship. Mrs. Schmidt graciously allowed Jim to replace her at the organ. It wasn't long before Jim and Beth were regular helpers there.[53]

---

[52] The *Trinity Hymnal* was first published in 1961 by Great Commission Publications of the Orthodox Presbyterian Church. It has since been revised, and its original blue cover has been replaced with red. The "Red Trinity" is used widely in Reformed churches, including the Presbyterian Church in America. "Trinity Hymnal Resources," https://www.opc.org/ hymnal.html (accessed September 9, 2017). The "Blue Trinity" is still in use at NCF Chattanooga.

[53] *New City Fellowship—Brief History*, p.3.

James Ward

So welcome, James Ward.[54] He and Randy Nabors were classmates at Covenant College, Class of 1972. Jim played the piano, sang, and composed. When Collyn Schmidt relinquished the portable Hammond organ to Jim, she apparently made a good decision, because as of this writing Jim is still in charge of music at NCF Chattanooga, and it's almost 50 years down the track. Ward's ingenious melding of traditional black and traditional white music has proven to be integral and indispensable to the ministry of New City, and to the greater church as well.[55]

Inner-City Missions

On February 3, 1972, twenty-two Third Street Sunday School participants and supporters met to discuss the ministry's status, needs and plans for expansion. The agenda for the meeting is set out in the minutes, recorded by James Ward: "Purpose: business, what has happened, what is happening, and what should happen." As to "present situation," the minutes read:

> Third St. Sunday School is still in the same apt. Much improved but still deficient. Church has grown. Sunday School and Church have been crammed. Adults have not responded. Teen-agers are growing up. No transportation. Need a new building and a van.[56]

The group decided to incorporate a separate organization called "Inner-City Missions"; a checking account had already been opened under the mistaken name "*Inter*-City Missions." (The minutes note that "Randy liked that idea of expanded work.")

---

[54] See chapter 6, "The Songmaker."

[55] Two of Ward's hymns appear in the "Red" *Trinity Hymnal*, "Morning Sun" (hymn 287) and his arrangement of "Rock of Ages" (hymn 500). *Trinity Hymnal*, Suwanee, GA: Great Commission Publications, Inc. (1995).

[56] "Inner-City Missions Organizational Meeting—February 3, 1972" (minutes), p.2.

One reason for the establishment of Inner-City Missions was that it had become difficult for Lookout Mountain RPC to administer the mission's business on its own. A fireman from Chattanooga named Dave Mitchell, for example, had donated a car to the ministry. It had to be registered in Randy's name because there was no other legal entity available. And later, with the need to sign leases and purchase property, a separate legal entity was also essential.

Another reason to incorporate was financial support for the work. By this time, there were needs that couldn't be met by one church alone. Other churches besides Lookout Mountain RPC had already begun to chip in, such as First Baptist and First Presbyterian, both in the city of Chattanooga, and Lookout Mountain Presbyterian, the latter two at that time still member churches of the Southern Presbyterian denomination. Individual donors needed to be able to give directly to the work as well.

In addition to the decision to establish the work and to incorporate, the group discussed possible programs for outreach on a wider scale, including work with so-called street people: alcoholics, addicts and prostitutes. The participants at the meeting had more vision than means. They wanted an urban Christian center with a thrift store, tutoring and reading classes, a day school and a coffeehouse. They wanted a weekly club for neighborhood kids, including music, rollerskating, swimming and camping programs, with scholarships available. They saw a need for increased street evangelism and Bible studies—all of this while looking for a new venue since the Third Street apartment was too small.

However, the establishment of Inner-City Missions did not end the ministry's ecclesiastical connection to Reformed Presbyterian Church of Lookout Mountain. That church still provided a borrowed session, and the session continued to lead the ministry as a mission church up though New City Fellowship's particularization in 1976.[57]

Move to Mitchell Avenue

The same Jim Ward who recorded the minutes would soon be recording music and needed a place to rehearse. One place he checked out was Chattanooga's Southside YMCA on Mitchell Avenue. Griff Long, a "Y" staff member, offered him a room that needed cleaning and painting, and that worked for Jim. It worked for Long too, who had been looking for some way to put the "Christian" back into Young Men's Christian Association. After getting permission from the YMCA board, Jim (for practice) and Inner-City Missions (for worship) were both invited to use the facility. The Southside Y was located on Mitchell Avenue, about a mile and a half from the apartment building where Third Street had been meeting.

It seemed spacious at the time, but the church continued to grow. Within three years the "pink YMCA" (due to its exterior paint) meant cramped worship services once again. More space was needed, and the session[58] decided to supplement by purchasing a building right next to the Y. That became known as "Fellowship House." Only a day after the decision was made to buy the property, a friend came forward with the exact amount needed for the down payment.[59] Together, the "pink" YMCA and the Fellowship House on Mitchell Avenue would remain NCF's site until 1984.

Ed & Doreen Kellogg

In 1973, five years after Third Street Sunday School opened its doors, Ed and Doreen Kellogg joined the ministry. They had

---

[57] See p.63.

[58] By this time, Lookout Mountain RPC had appointed some ruling elders from LMRPC to act as a session for NCF, under the authority of the LMRPC session as a whole.

[59] *New City Fellowship—Brief History*, p.4.

already been sensitized to the need for racial reconciliation in the church. Ed remembers that when he was 9 years old, C. Herbert Oliver, an African-American pastor and graduate of Westminster Theological Seminary, came with his family to dinner at the Kellogg home in West Collingswood, NJ. Oliver had personally experienced racial violence in Birmingham, Alabama during the late 1950s and early 1960s. He had authored the book *No Flesh Shall Glory*[60] in which he denounced the evil of individual prejudice as the root cause of racism, as opposed to structural or institutional discrimination. In the years following his visit with the Kelloggs, Oliver sent pamphlets on the civil rights movement to Ed's father, and Ed read them.

In 1954, when Ed was 10, his family moved to San Diego. When young "Eddie," in his mid-teens, became president of the youth group in his family's church there, he took it upon himself to read some of the Oliver pamphlets and newsletters to the group. Doreen, born and raised in San Diego, was a member of the youth group, and what Ed was sharing resonated with her—one of her grandparent's racial comments had always bothered her. The youth group helped her gain a biblical perspective on the subject.

The young teens didn't merely listen to what Oliver had to say. They spent time praying for the Lord to make his love and justice known in the racial unrest and violence boiling over in America at the time. So when the Kelloggs came to NCF in 1973,[61] they had already learned a good deal about how crucial it was to deal with race issues. And they meant to get involved personally.

Both Ed and Doreen are artists. Ed was head of Covenant College's art department and continued on the college faculty through 2010. Doreen's artistic gift has been expressed mostly

---

[60] Oliver, C. Herbert, *No Flesh Shall Glory*. Nutley, NJ: Presbyterian & Reformed Publishing (1959).
[61] Doreen and Ed had married in August 1965 while living in San Diego.

through her design of "worship banners" some of which have become icons, in the best sense, at New City. Ed's oil paintings are heavy with creation's features: trees, rocks, blooms and foliage predominate. His goal isn't to preach, but to fairly represent what he sees "out there." But in doing so, his work cannot help but "preach." It displays the beauty of God's *general* revelation in creation. Doreen's work draws more on God's *special* revelation in scripture:[62] "Banners are not just decorations but reminders of God's grace as revealed in the Bible. They are declarations of his revealed truth."[63]

Doreen's work has been front and center at New City. She's the one who did NCF's original logo, three racially diverse hands grasping the Cross. In November 2001, in celebration of NCF's 25th anniversary, eight of Doreen's textile hangings were placed in the sanctuary. The hangings are antiphonal graphics: there are four "declarations" each with its counterpart "response." The four themes are God's Love, God's Faithfulness, God's Righteousness and God's Justice.[64] These four sets represented a kind of milestone for Doreen, but she has continued her art ministry to the present, with this objective: *"May these banners enrich and beautify the worship space of New City Fellowship and may they bring glory to the Lord of Creation."*[65]

---

[62] The *Belgic Confession* (1561), Article 2, reads: "We know Him [God] by two means: First, by the creation, preservation, and government of the universe; which is before our eyes as a most elegant book, wherein all creatures, great and small, are as so many characters leading us to *see clearly the invisible things of God*, even *his everlasting power and divinity,* as the apostle Paul says in Romans 1:20. All which things are sufficient to convince men and leave them without excuse. Second, He makes Himself more clearly and fully known to us by His holy and divine Word, that is to say, as far as is necessary for us to know in this life, to His glory and our salvation."

[63] Personal interviews with Ed and Doreen Kellogg, August 9, 2017.

[64] In keeping with Doreen's commitment to draw on Scripture, all of the declarations and responses are direct quotes. For example, the "Love" pair: *Declaration*: "Your love O LORD reaches to the heavens"; *Response*: "How great is the love the Father has lavished on us (that we should be called children of God)". *The Sanctuary Banners*, leaflet (November, 2001).

[65] Ibid.

New City's Name

In 1976, when the congregation and borrowed session were searching for an appropriate name for the new church, Ed Kellogg suggested "New City." He had been studying the book of Jeremiah and was taken with this verse in which the prophet exhorted the Jewish remnant about what they were to do when they arrived in Babylon: "But seek the welfare of the city where I have sent you into exile, and pray to the LORD on its behalf, for in its welfare you will find your welfare." (Jer. 29:7).

So, Ed reasoned, if we are an integral part of God's redemptive work in the city into which we are sent—specifically, Chattanooga—our welfare is divinely wrapped up in Chattanooga's welfare. The work we are called to is in solidarity with Chattanooga in the same way that the Jewish exiles were in solidarity with the citizenry of Babylon. Our work, like theirs, is transformational, ultimately resulting in the true (presently invisible) "new city"—the New Jerusalem described in Revelation 21. And thus our name should be a statement of faith, identical to the faith of Abraham: "For he was looking forward to the city that has foundations, whose designer and builder is God." [66]

The additional word "Fellowship" was added to convey a warm Christian welcome to the community. Ed and others were aware of its use in St. Louis by a church in the RPCES, Grace & Peace Fellowship, and liked it.

Development of Black Leadership

By the spring of 1972, Randy Nabors was shouldering most of the preaching duties. The mission church was growing. Staff and students from Covenant College were much attracted to the ministry, many holding their membership at Lookout Mountain RPC but attending worship services downtown. Some of the college students were African-American, and by summer 1973, a nucleus of black leadership had emerged. But that was also

---
[66] Heb. 11:10.

the summer that Randy left for ministerial training at Covenant Seminary in St. Louis. During that three-year stint, running from mid-1973 through mid-1976, existing NCF leadership and a Bible professor from Covenant College, Chuck Anderson, managed the preaching. The work continued to grow.

It wasn't without growing pains, though. From late 1975 through spring 1976, a dispute arose between some of the newer black leaders and the white leaders who had been there since the beginning in 1968. A major issue was whether the ministry should continue under a presbyterian form of government—specifically, under the authority of Lookout Mountain RPC and the RPCES[67]—or become independent. But Rodney Alexander, an African American from Newark who had been with the ministry from almost the beginning,[68] intervened.

A graduate of Covenant College and now a Covenant Seminary student, Rod sacrificially took a year off from his seminary studies to provide leadership. Recognizing the importance of accountability as practiced in the presbyterian form of church governance, he helped to quell the concern of those who thought that remaining in the RPCES would be too restrictive. Additionally, he believed that "we should dance with who brung us," that is, the Reformed Presbyterian Church on Lookout Mountain, which had supported the work from the beginning. The call for independence waned, and the ministry remained in the RPCES.

Randy Nabors Called; Particularization

However, when Rodney Alexander returned to Covenant Seminary in the fall of 1976, it became clear that NCF was in need of pastoral leadership. Two elders, Ed Kellogg and Rudy Schmidt, traveled to St. Louis to urge Randy Nabors (just finish-

---

[67] By early 1976 New City Chattanooga had been adopted as a mission church of Southern Presbytery, RPCES.
[68] See p.45.

ing seminary training himself) to come back to Chattanooga.[69] He did, and in November 1976 the Southern Presbytery (PCA), which had ordained Randy as a teaching elder in June of that year, held a service installing Randy as pastor and "particularizing"[70] NCF as an independent church. It would no longer be a mission under the auspices of Lookout Mountain RPC or Southern Presbytery.

Music Ministry

So New City Fellowship Chattanooga was on its own, and in good hands with Randy Nabors as senior pastor. But a crucial component of the ministry had been interrupted while Randy was away at seminary. In 1975, Jim and Beth Ward had moved from Chattanooga to spend time at Camp Peniel and environs in upstate New York where Jim helped organize a band and toured. NCF was without his leadership in the music ministry for almost three years. During this break, Bryan Holland began to put together a choir and served as director of music.[71] Jim, however, was no wandering minstrel and the Wards returned to Chattanooga in April of 1978:

> [Jim] again took up the duties of music ministry in the church. He was paid a small stipend, but continued to tour so he was gone some Sundays. A tremendous volume of new and original music developed at New City. Eventually a song book for New City was printed and in 1982 the choir produced a cassette recording, *Songs of the New City*. Some of the songs written by Jim came to be printed in the *Trinity* and other hymnals. This helped create an atmosphere for musical skill and gifts to flourish.

---

[69] See p.49.

[70] A "particular" church can exist only after being constituted by presbytery, and is self-governing, electing its own session and diaconate.

[71] *2001: 25th Anniversary, New City Fellowship at Westminster*, p.4.

Other New City musicians, such as Leland Stewart, also wrote music for the church.[72]

Kenya Interlude

Randy Nabors was still senior pastor when, in 1982, he and Joan accepted an invitation to go to Kenya to pastor the Community Presbyterian Church in Nairobi. The New City session reluctantly agreed to a two-year appointment to that mission field. They were hesitant to leave their pulpit empty for so long, but happily the Lord provided Carl Ellis. An African American, Carl was a graduate of Westminster Seminary and a former Senior Campus Minister with Tom Skinner Associates in New York. He was available to fill NCF's pulpit during the two years when Randy and Joan were gone.[73]

Move to Chattanooga Christian School

When Joan and Randy returned in 1984, the church was still meeting at the YMCA and Fellowship House on Mitchell Avenue. But serious problems were developing with the Y's gym. The congregation had done what they could aesthetically—painting it and hanging Doreen Kellogg's banners[74]—but when the heating system broke down, the cost of fixing it was too much. When the congregants had to resort to overcoats and blankets one Sunday morning, it became obvious that NCF needed a bet-

---

[72] *New City Fellowship—Brief History*, p.4. One of Stewart's best-known compositions is his arrangement of Robert Lowry's 1876 hymn, "Nothing but the Blood."

[73] See pp.66ff. As of this writing, Ellis holds a Master of Arts in Religion degree from Westminster Seminary and D.Phil. from Oxford Graduate School. He has served on the faculty at Chesapeake Theological Seminary, as adjunct faculty member at the Center for Urban Theological Studies in Philadelphia, and as Dean of Intercultural Studies at Westminster Seminary. He presently is on faculty at Reformed Theological Seminary as Assistant to the Chancellor, Senior Fellow of the African American Leadership Initiative, and Provost's Professor of Theology and Culture. Reformed Theological Seminary: Faculty and Staff, https://www.rts.edu/seminary/faculty/bio.aspx?id=665 (accessed October 16, 2018).

[74] See p.60.

ter facility. The next Sunday, in early 1985, they began meeting in the commons at Chattanooga Christian School on Charger Drive, about two miles southwest of the YMCA. The church continued to meet there for the next five years and saw consistent growth in membership, outreach and ministry.

Home Sweet Home: Westminster

A permanent building had to be found for this growing congregation. NCF's session put together a five-year plan, scheduling a move to a permanent facility in no more than three years. They almost made it. Westminster Presbyterian Church,[75] located at 2412 East Fourth Street in downtown Chattanooga, agreed to transfer its property to NCF in exchange for a $300,000 trust fund for support of missionaries and staff retirement. The agreement was signed at a joint meeting of the two congregations on New Year's Eve, 1989. New City could start 1990 in a spacious, colonial style building (with actual pews!)—and they would own it.

Desert Storm;
Barry Henning and Carl Ellis

In 1990 Randy was called up for duty as an Army chaplain during Desert Storm. Barry Henning, an ordained teaching elder in the PCA, assumed the duties though not the title of senior pastor. He, his wife Ann and family[76] had become fixtures at NCF beginning in the summer of 1987, when the church was meeting at Chattanooga Christian School. When Randy returned at the end of May, 1991, Barry wanted to stay on the pastoral staff. And many congregants, having profited from his ministry, felt the same way.

But the leadership at NCF couldn't create slots for everyone and was firmly committed to the pursuit of another priority: Af-

---

[75] Westminster, like NCF, was a member church of the Presbyterian Church in America.

[76] See chapter 8.

rican-American leadership. Whatever else might be said about Barry Henning, he wasn't African-American, and so he didn't fit the plan:

> There was a period of some confusion, but all of the leadership agreed—black pastoral staff was essential for New City's mission.[77]

Barry did stay on part-time at NCF, and shortly after Randy Nabors' return from Desert Storm, was asked to fill the pulpit at Lookout Mountain Reformed Presbyterian Church, NCF's original sponsor. He accepted and continued this work for a year until he and his family moved to St. Louis in the summer of 1992, fulfilling their earlier commitment.[78]

The leadership of NCF followed through on their commitment to employ an African American on the pastoral staff. In summer 1992, Carl Ellis accepted a call as associate pastor. There was some controversy over the calling of a black associate—not due to any concerns about Ellis—but because not everyone agreed that a person should be hired based on the color of his skin. However, leadership was convinced that in a cross-cultural church with an outreach to African Americans, such a qualification was important.[79] More than that, Ellis was highly qualified for the position in every other way. Moreover, he had subbed for Randy Nabors in the pulpit from 1982-84. This time around, he would serve as associate pastor for a little over two years.

EXPANSION OF CHURCH MINISTRIES

NCF's move to the Westminster property on East Fourth Street in January 1990 had triggered a significant growth spurt, both in number of congregants and in funds available for ministry. Needed staff was added. An ordained teaching elder, Jim Pickett, was hired to head the youth ministry and was later pro-

---

[77] *New City Fellowship—Brief History*, p.6.
[78] See pp.93ff.
[79] *New City Fellowship—Brief History*, p.6.

moted to associate pastor for youth, visitation and assimilation. Paul Green became director of children's ministry, Chris Hatch was appointed as director of community economic development, and just to keep everyone organized and on track, Patsy Owens was hired as administrative assistant.[80]

But the church didn't get swallowed up in its own bureaucracy. Focus on the original purposes of the church was maintained. Even during the days of Third Street Sunday School, a ministry had been created for widows in the neighborhood who needed assistance financially. To coordinate this work, a separate entity was formed: Chattanooga Widows Harvest Ministry. New City was so committed to the ministry that the church donated Fellowship House on Mitchell to the new organization. The ministry's work has been aided greatly by teams of young people from other churches across the country volunteering as a temporary labor force to help with home repairs. This vital ministry continues to this day.

To make room for expanding staff and requisite office space, the church purchased a house adjacent to the Westminster sanctuary on Fourth Street. It needed renovation but proved to be an important aid in both reaching out to the community and ministering to the body of believers, two needs which seem to grow in tandem in a healthy church.

Hope For The Inner City

Ministry to the poor, of course, has always been front and center at NCF Chattanooga. The diaconate maintains casework to determine where true need exists, and also works through Hope for the Inner City, an organization whose board consists of NCF members. The board's stated goal is,

> "...to bring hope...to targeted communities by offering Christ-centered programs and services to meet the physi-

---
[80] Ibid., p.7.

cal, spiritual and social development needs of individuals and families [and thus to restore the] dignity of Chattanooga's inner-city residents through the reconciliation of our communities to God through Jesus Christ."[81]

They have been targeting East Chattanooga, the city's poorest area, and want to see it emerge as:

A revitalized place where chronic homelessness gives way to permanent housing.

A re-energized place where poverty gives way to prosperity.

A reconciled place where broken families learn to live in harmony with each other.

A restored place where dilapidated properties turn into friendly streets.

A redeemed place where violent gang members re-emerge as productive citizens.

Reaching these essential goals, they believe, will be greatly aided as suburban Christians, compelled by the gospel of Christ, form deep friendships with their inner-city neighbors.[82]

Mike Higgins

In 1997 another ordained teaching elder, Mike Higgins, entered the picture at NCF Chattanooga as associate pastor. Like Randy Nabors and Jim Pickett, he was a graduate of Covenant Seminary; like Carl Ellis, he was African-American.

The Higgins family became instantly and fully active in nearly every facet of NCF's ministry. They were particularly gifted in music and, in addition, Mike assumed special responsibility for engaging young African-American men in the work of the

---

[81] *Hope for the Inner City: Mission and Vision*, https://www.hopefortheinnercity.org/mission-vision/ (accessed August 27, 2018).

[82] *The New City Network: Hope for the Inner City*, https://www.thenewcitynetwork.org/bridgeport-chattanooga.html (accessed August 27, 2018).

church. During another sabbatical for Randy and Joan Nabors in 1999, Mike replaced Randy as moderator of the session. Soon after, in 2000, the session agreed to let Higgins go for a period of time at his request to preach at an African-American church, Redemption Fellowship in Atlanta. Redemption had asked for NCF's assistance, having lost their pastor and having experienced some turmoil as a result. NCF continued to pay Mike Higgins' salary while he filled Redemption's pulpit.[83]

Leadership Challenge

Mike Higgins' departure left a gap at the church, and so the session employed an African-American intern, Marvin Williams, to cover for Mike for the next two years. But Marvin and his wife Rowena, deeply interested in church planting and carrying with them the New City vision, left to plant an African-American congregation in Dallas. The pastoral gap at NCF widened when Paul Green, director of children's ministry, accepted a call to become director of Hope for Chattanooga (later Hope for the Inner City). And Chris Hatch with his wife Josephine left for St. Louis to prepare for a church planting mission in London.

Then 9/11 happened. Randy Nabors, still a reserve chaplain, was once more called up for active duty in the Army. Even though stationed more than 100 miles away in Atlanta, he was able to continue preaching at NCF intermittently. Now more staff was needed, but it was difficult to hire because the 2002 budget "was a very difficult one."[84] Some staff members were laid off. Attendance declined somewhat.

---

[83] In 1992 Higgins and his wife Renee later relocated from Chattanooga to St. Louis, their hometown, where Mike joined the staff at Covenant Seminary as Dean of Students. He also serves as senior pastor at South City Church (PCA) in St. Louis, a separate church from New City Fellowship South, though a member of New City Network (see ch. 9). Mike and Renee's daughter Michelle is Director of Worship and Outreach at South City Church. *South City Church: Staff & Leadership*: http://www.southcitychurch.com/home/staff/ (accessed August 15, 2018).

[84] *New City Fellowship—Brief History*, p.8.

Kingdom-Builders

Teaching elder Jim Pickett was associate pastor during this time and did most of the preaching. In an effort to inject new life into the church, Jim worked with the session, and together they:

> ...decided on a more aggressive approach in bringing new members into a fuller involvement in the life of the church. They established a program called "Kingdom Builders," through which ruling elders link up with each new members class and follow that group into a progressive experience of discipleship, fellowship, and ministry over three years.[85]

By fall 2004 the church had hired a new director of Christian education, Randy Jackson. Jackson was able to hire part-time junior and senior high staff. A summer day camp was established, and the original urban camp, which had ceased for a time, resumed. In 2005 NCF established The Lighthouse, a community house in the neighborhood near Memorial Hospital, and staff was again added through the organizational skill of Christy Graeber, office administrator.

Death of Rudolph Schmidt

"Uncle Rudy" Schmidt, formerly registrar at Covenant College and ruling elder at NCF from 1968 on, died suddenly in November 2005. For 37 years Rudy had consistently modeled what it meant to be an urban worker: pursuing Bible studies in members' homes, tutoring children, giving new attendees a joyful greeting (and remembering their names), tending to the finances of the church, loving and delighting in the ministries of African Americans in the church, and always supporting (sometimes defending) the pastor though the years.

His wife Collyn continued much of what Rudy had done until she died at age 92 in the fall of 2016. The Schmidts had been

---

[85] Ibid., p.8.

with NCF since its beginning in 1968 when the Third Street Sunday School was established.[86] The session had never been without Rudy. He had been a stabilizing influence, and his death left a hole in NCF's sessional leadership, but by 2005 the session and church as a whole were well equipped to sustain the loss.

Thirtieth Anniversary

Fall 2006 meant time for celebration. NCF Chattanooga was officially 30 years old as a particular church. Mike Higgins, still preaching regularly at Redemption Fellowship in Atlanta, was the featured speaker at a celebratory banquet held at the Chattanoogan Hotel on Broad Street. Only a few months later, in January 2007, NCF purchased a manse across from the church building at 2505 Fifth Street. Randy and Joan Nabors moved in and continued to occupy that residence up until Randy's resignation as senior pastor in 2010.

Wy Plummer

In 2008, NCF was able to call another African American, Wy Plummer, first as a staff pastor and then as an executive pastor. Wy owns a bachelor's degree from Howard University, a graduate degree from Johns Hopkins, and his M.Div. from Chesapeake Reformed Theological Seminary. He was ordained into the PCA in 1995. As of this writing he wears multiple hats: in addition to his position at NCF Chattanooga, he is a member of the advisory board of Covenant Seminary and coordinator of Mission to North America's African-American Ministries.

Jim & Michele Pickett

Jim Pickett was born and raised in Las Cruces, New Mexico. He grew up on a farm 50 miles from the Mexican border, and by the age of five he was speaking Spanish. His parents

---
[86] See pp.33ff.

took him to a Las Cruces Episcopal church, but Jim claims that he never heard the gospel there. His older brother John had become a Christian, however, and in the summer of 1970, after Jim graduated from high school, John shared the gospel with him. In December of that year the two attended Inter-Varsity Christian Fellowship's annual conference in Urbana, Illinois. It was there that Jim fully came to receive Christ as his Savior.

Jim graduated in 1975 from the University of Oklahoma with a B.A. in Latin American history and was now fluent in Spanish. His plan was to be a high school history teacher and football coach. But he was conflicted, and contacted Francis Schaeffer (as many conflicted souls did in that generation) to see if he should come to L'Abri Fellowship in Switzerland to try to sort things out. Schaeffer suggested that he might be better advised to give Covenant Seminary a try, and that he might look into attending Grace & Peace Fellowship while in St. Louis. Jim took Schaeffer's advice.

He enrolled at Covenant in the fall of 1975. He attended for three semesters—half-way through the three year regimen—and though he enjoyed Old Testament studies and Hebrew, he was not happy with the seminary track as a whole. Ceasing seminary studies for a time, he became increasingly involved at Grace & Peace, eventually becoming part of that church's plant in the heart of poverty-stricken North St. Louis City: Murphy Blair Community Church. He was elected and ordained a ruling elder at Murphy Blair. Jim found this work in a cross-cultural setting fulfilling, and with encouragement from friends he returned to Covenant, graduating with his M.Div. in 1981.

Jim now knew that he wanted to work in an urban setting and was glad to be asked to come to a successfully planted PCA church in Manhattan—not Redeemer, but assisted by some of Redeemer's members—which had recently hit rough waters. Jim traveled to New York, liked the core group of people, accepted the call and for six years worked toward the renewal of that church. Longing for yet more cross-cultural experience, he then accepted a call to Covenant PCA, a Chinese church in Queens, to work with their American born, young adult membership. It was during this time that he met Michele Albury, a doctor just finishing her residency at Mt. Sinai Hospital in New York City. The M.Div. and the M.D. married in November of 1993.

Jim and Michele were interested in planting a new multi-cultural PCA church in New York. Seeking guidance, Jim called Randy Nabors. That may have been a mistake. Just two weeks later NCF Chattanooga contacted Jim and conveyed Randy's wish that Jim and Michele would consider coming to NCF Chattanooga. After some soul-searching, the Picketts came to believe that God was calling them to NCF. In 1994 they visited Chattanooga, and the Lord's leading was confirmed to them when Michele, after an interview lasting less than ten minutes, was offered a position on the pediatric faculty of the University of Tennessee Medical Center at Erlanger Hospital in Chattanooga.

Jim made an initial commitment for three years, but it turned out to be a considerably longer relationship. He remained NCF's associate pastor from 1994 up through 2016. In 2007 he and Michele briefly considered a move west, possibly to San Diego to work with Dick Kauffman in church planting there. Jim was excited, however, by the possibility of a new church plant to be established in an area of Chattanooga known as East Lake.

NEW CITY EAST LAKE

New City's session had always been committed to planting a second church in Chattanooga as soon as possible after membership reached 500, and that goal had been met. In the fall of 2008, under Jim Pickett's leadership and coordinated with NCF and Tennessee Valley Presbytery, the new church was born: New City East Lake, about three miles north of NCF Chattanooga. Teaching elder Al Lutz, himself a career church planter in the PCA, had retired to Lookout Mountain and was able to provide valuable advice and leadership in the early stages of the new work. A formal "commissioning" service was held at East Lake Academy in November 2009. To distinguish the two congregations, both located in Chattanooga, the original Westminster site became known as "New City Fellowship Glenwood" and the new church plant as "New City East Lake." Presbytery particularized the new church in September 2016, installing Pickett as senior pastor.

Testimonies are myriad of Christians who find, at the time they are called to a specific ministry, that the Lord had prepared them for that ministry much earlier though they didn't have a clue about it at the time. In this case a younger Jim had become fluent in Spanish as a boy and studied Latin American history in the early 1970's. Now in 2012, 40 years later, New City East Lake is approximately 20 percent Latino. The Lord not only knows but declares "...the end from the beginning."[87]

Kevin & Sandra Smith

If way back three decades ago, the Lord had appeared in a vision and told New City/PCA to appoint a search committee to scout for a young African-American preacher to fill a need in the church in Chattanooga, it seems unlikely that they would have looked in a Church of God—a church in the Pentecostal tradition that takes serious exception to many of the teachings of Reformed theology. It's doubtful that West Oak Lane Church of God, then located in Northern Philadelphia, would even have been contacted. But that's where they would have found Kevin Smith, who since 2012 has served as NCF Glenwood's senior pastor.

Kevin grew up in a lower middle class area in Philadelphia. His dad worked as a construction foreman. In March 1981, when Kevin was 17 years old, a friend, Craig Cadwell, led him to Christ. He began to fellowship regularly at West Oak Lane Church of God. In 1982, Kevin enrolled at Temple University in

---

[87] Isa. 46:10.

Philadelphia and in 1987 graduated with a degree in therapeutic recreation. He also met Sandra Brown.

Sandra was born in Jamaica, her family moving to the Philadelphia area when she was just seven years old, in second grade. By the way, if that search committee had also been commissioned to look for a pastor's wife, they would probably not have scheduled an appointment at the Roman Catholic Archdiocese of Philadelphia, but Sandra was born into the Roman Catholic Church in Jamaica and went to mass regularly until she was in middle school in Philadelphia. At that time she and her sister found a Baptist church right across the alley from the family's home, which, with their father's permission, both of them began to attend.

In the summer of 1987, Sandra and Kevin married, degrees from Temple in hand. Hers was in marketing and economics. They were married at, and were still attending, West Oak Lane Church of God. Both had jobs: Kevin as a counselor at Philadelphia Psychiatric Center, and Sandra as an intern at the U.S. Department of Defense. But both realized that Kevin was being called into the ministry, and that such jobs were likely going to be temporary.

During this time, the two attended a Sunday school class at West Oak. An associate pastor taught it, and it was basically a critique of "TULIP,"[88] a well-known acronym said to summarize the substance of Calvinistic reformed theology, as opposed to Arminianism. The pastor taught TULIP as a "hellish doctrine," but as Kevin and Sandra listened, Calvin's theology seemed to coordinate with scripture, and it resonated with them. The Smiths' movement toward reformed thinking was stimulated as they began to read the writings of John MacArthur and Martin Lloyd Jones. Kevin also read Edwin H. Palmer's well-known book, *The*

---

[88] Also termed by some as the "Five Points of Calvinism": Total Depravity, Unconditional Election, Limited Atonement, Irresistible Grace and Perseverance of the Saints.

Five Points of Calvinism, and began to "take ownership" of the doctrines of grace which are central to reformed theology.

James Montgomery Boice was pastor of Tenth Presbyterian Church in Philadelphia (PCA) at the time, and Kevin was particularly helped spiritually as he listened to Boice's radio series on the book of Romans—so much so that the Smiths joined Tenth PC. In 1990, convinced of his call to the ministry, Kevin enrolled at Westminster Seminary in Philadelphia and in 1991 became a pastoral intern at Tenth, working under Boice.

Kevin's ability both in preaching and counseling were obvious, and Philadelphia Presbytery paid his seminary tuition. He was taken under care of Philadelphia Presbytery and finished his seminary training at Chesapeake Reformed Theological Seminary in Maryland. He was then called to a new church plant in Bowie, Maryland, a few miles west of Washington D.C. Potomac Presbytery sponsored the new church, and the Smiths continued there for seven years, 1998-2005. Meanwhile they started a family, and God has blessed them with four girls.

In 2005 the Smiths moved to Miami, answering a call from Pineland Presbyterian Church (PCA). The congregation was multicultural: Latinos, Caucasians, Caribbeans and African Americans.

The Smiths were happy there, and the church was prospering, but in 2011 they got a telephone call from NCF Chattanooga. Randy Nabors had stepped away from the senior pastor spot, and the "now hiring" sign was up in the front window. Kevin's immediate response was no. He didn't feel qualified. But NCF was persistent, and at the same time Niel Nielson, then president of Covenant College, asked Kevin to speak at a special lecture series at the Lookout Mountain campus.[89]

---

[89] When the Smiths came to Lookout Mountain, a member of the faculty at Covenant College and elder at NCF, Dr. Oliver Trimiew, collared Kevin and expressed his "upsetness" at Kevin's initial negative response to NCF's inquiry. Trimiew was one of the "Newark Quintet" of African Americans who

He and Sandra came, he lectured, and both attended a Sunday morning worship service at New City Glenwood. Sandra was blown away, not just by the worship service but also by the myriad mercy ministries in which NCF was engaged. As to worship style, at first they didn't know if they were a good fit since it was not what they were used to, but they were confident that they meshed perfectly with the central message and ministries of this PCA "mother-ship" of outreach to the poor and racial reconciliation. That was what was important; it was what they really wanted to do. With the Lord's help, they concluded, they could.

So Kevin accepted the call as senior pastor and preached his first Sunday morning service at NCF Glenwood on July 8, 2012. At this writing he continues in that position. Randy Nabors had been senior pastor for 40 years. If Kevin matches that, he'll celebrate his retirement from NCF on July 7, 2052.

Third Street Sunday School: Mission Accomplished

The people who had started Third Street Sunday School in 1968, forty-four years earlier, could rejoice. Many of them, like Rudy Schmidt, had gone to heaven, and they were surely rejoicing as well.[90] A major milestone had been reached in 2012: the calling of an African-American senior pastor.[91] Though color of skin never qualifies someone as pastor, it does certify that the church is fully committed to minority leadership. This, in turn,

---

enrolled at Covenant College in Fall, 1968 (see p.45). He knew firsthand what the vision was for the church when it was Third Street Sunday School half a century earlier, what people there had been hoping and praying for, and saw Kevin as an answer to those prayers and fulfillment of that vision.

[90] "After this I looked, and behold, a great multitude that no one could number, from every nation, from all tribes and peoples and languages, standing before the throne and before the Lamb, clothed in white robes, with palm branches in their hands, and crying out with a loud voice, 'Salvation belongs to our God who sits on the throne, and to the Lamb!' " (Rev. 7:9-10).

[91] See p.45. In 1968, Third Street Sunday School had set as a high priority the seeking out of a full-time black minister.

promotes outreach to African Americans and other minority communities. It belies "tokenism" and demonstrates that a nearly all-white denomination like the Presbyterian Church in America can indeed be serious about racial reconciliation and integration within the Body of Christ. It gives believers the confidence that it *can happen*—not just theoretically—but in real time.[92]

Church Ministries

A large number of ministries does not necessarily mean that true biblical ministry is being done in a church. But it can mean that a wholehearted effort is being made to obey the demands of the gospel. New City in Chattanooga, at this writing, has these effective particular ministries, instituted because of evident need:

First Sunday Prayer Meeting. All of NCF's work and ministry start here. At 5 p.m., first Sunday of each month, NCF members gather for prayer—not just for their church, but for their field of mission: the City of Chattanooga. "And work for the peace and prosperity of the city where I sent you into exile. Pray to the Lord for it, for its welfare will determine your welfare." (Jer. 29:7).

Small Groups. NCF Chattanooga is no longer fourteen children and a few adults meeting in an apartment. Perhaps the early Third Street Sunday School was its own original "small group," but the church has since grown to many hundreds of believers. It's impossible for one member to know all the others. By forming small cell groups, meeting weekly for fellowship, Bible study and prayer, NCF encourages an intimacy and sense of belonging that just isn't possible in a larger arena. NCF has about a dozen such groups in the greater Chattanooga area.

---

[92] See Appendix 11, "Is An Integrated Church Possible?"

Missions. NCF's missions committee oversees the church's relationship with and funding for missionaries the church supports, some in foreign countries and some stateside. Mission priorities are consistent with the vision owned by NCF from its origin: (1) a desire to see more African-American missionaries, particularly in international postings under qualified mission boards; (2) supporting missionaries who reflect the particular vision of NCF in their lives both at home and overseas; (3) selection of target areas where the vision of NCF can best be expressed, working with partner churches and other ministries; and (4) where possible, engaging persons who have been active in the ministry of NCF long enough to demonstrate a commitment to its values and priorities, including the pursuit of racial diversity in the church. "Missions Emphasis Week" is an annual occurrence at New City, where attendees hear speakers, participate in panel discussions, and eat together (with maybe a Congolese, Kenyan or Nepalese menu), all with the objective of increasing understanding of and participation in missions.[93]

GLAD and Community Outreach. As discussed in chapter 3 of this book, little children comprised the first meetings of what became New City. They were loved with the love of Jesus, warmly welcomed and treated as precious individuals. That welcoming, loving spirit continues at NCF Chattanooga.

Through "GLAD" (Glenwood Learning Adventure Days) elementary school children are tutored in math and reading four days a week during the school year. Although tutoring requires consistency and at times can be challenging, tutors find it rewarding. GLAD is volunteer

---

[93] "New City Fellowship Missions," http://www.newcityfellowship.com/missions (accessed June 22, 2018).

based and promotes caring relationships between tutor and child. In the summer, when the program transforms into "Camp Glad" day camp, tutoring continues, but the children also participate in athletic activities, swimming, crafts and outings.

Deacons' Mercy Ministry. The diaconate at NCF Chattanooga is composed of both men and women. In keeping with the New Testament's teachings regarding diaconal qualifications and role in the church,[94] NCF describes deacons' responsibilities (in addition to caring for the church's property) as ministering to those who are needy, sick, friendless, or in distress. Resources are always limited, and so the diaconate is also charged with challenging the congregation to "develop the grace of liberality," to instill in each member a genuine, personal passion for those in need.[95]

New City Food Pantry. Sometimes families and individuals in Chattanooga, as in all communities, run out of food or money to purchase more. New City's Food Pantry provides emergency help for those who otherwise would go hungry until their next paycheck comes, if indeed a paycheck is coming. Those who visit the pantry are welcomed and supplied with food, of course, but they are also prayed for and encouraged to join in the regular worship of the church. This "cup of cold water" in Jesus' name has proven to be a powerful way to communicate the gospel.[96]

Anyone who doubts the efficacy of these kinds of mercy ministries need only ask Randy Nabors. His mom ran out of food and

---

[94] Acts 6:1-4; 1 Tim. 3:8-13.
[95] "New City Fellowship Deacons' Mercy Ministry," http://www.newcityfellowship.com/deacons-mercy-ministry (accessed June 23, 2018).
[96] "New City Fellowship Food Pantry Ministry," http://www.newcityfellowship.com/new-city-food-pantry-ministry (accessed June 23, 2018).

money in 1958. But through the timely generosity of the deacons from Calvary Gospel Church in Newark, not only did the family get what they needed to survive, but the whole Nabors family came to know Jesus as their Savior, including Randy.[97]

---

[97] See pp.40ff.

6.

THE SONGMAKER

*"O sing to the Lord a new song; sing to the Lord, all the earth!
Sing to the Lord, bless his name;
tell of his salvation from day to day."*—PSALM 96:1-2

JAMES CALVIN WARD was born and raised in Southern Illinois. His father, Samuel Ward, was longtime pastor at a Reformed Presbyterian Church, General Synod,[98] located in Coulterville, Illinois. The Coulterville pastorate lasted 17 years and was sandwiched between pastorates in Darlington, Pennsylvania, and Calvin Presbyterian Church in North Huntingdon, PA. Sam and his wife Rosalie were both musical, and their children—Keith, Jean, Mark, Paul, Timothy[99] and James—followed suit.

EARLY INFLUENCES

As a preacher's kid, Jim's upbringing meant singing from a hymnal, and the one used in the Ward household was the *Bi-*

---

[98] Samuel Ward attended Westminster Seminary in Philadelphia with Francis Schaeffer, John M.L. Young and John W. Sanderson, but finished his seminary education at the Reformed Presbyterian North America (RPCNA) Seminary in Pittsburgh. RPCNA permitted only psalmody in worship. Sam Ward did not have a conscientious objection to hymnody in worship, and thus chose to come under care of the Reformed Presbyterian Church, General Synod (RPCGS) which did not require exclusive psalmody. In 1965 the RPCGS united with the Evangelical Presbyterian Church, forming the Reformed Presbyterian Church, Evangelical Synod (RPCES).

[99] Timothy Carl Ward died in 1982 at age 26 of acute leukemia.

ble Songs Hymnal, published by the United Presbyterian Church of North America. That hymnal was a psalter, "a collection of psalms set to music."[100] It became the staple for the Ward family's singing around the dining room table, often accompanied by Rosalie or Jean at the piano. The *Bible Songs Hymnal* was also used in their church worship services.

But music in the Ward household was not limited to a hymnal, nor accompaniment to a piano. Sam played guitar in college and later switched to ukulele. He also enjoyed singing 1930's era pop and country western music. These diversions from the hymnal were important to Jim and the rest of the kids and gave them a wider appreciation for other music. Jim experimented with all kinds of music in high school and even began to compose some folk-style love songs.

Covenant College

In May of 1968 Jim graduated from Norwin High School, North Huntingdon, Pennsylvania. Because his father's church was now in the Reformed Presbyterian Church, Evangelical Synod, it was only natural that he'd attend the denomination's college on Lookout Mountain which four of his siblings had attended. He entered as a college freshman in fall of 1968. Being the son of a pastor, Jim thought briefly of entering the ministry himself, but recognized early on in his college days that his real love was music, and that's what he decided to pursue. So he majored in music, studying under John Hamm, the chair of the department, together with professors Noel McGee, John Canfield, Anita Jubin and Gary Huisman. Huisman taught him how to play the organ. Even though the music program at Covenant was limited to the classical and traditional, Jim recognized the importance of being grounded in these genres and thus earned his B.A. in mu-

---

[100] *Hymnary.org*, https://hymnary.org/denomination/455 (accessed September 18, 2017).

sic there in 1972. But even as an undergraduate he experimented with different forms.

Cultural Influences

The late '50s,'60s and early '70s brought enormous cultural change, particularly among America's youth. Racial strife was rampant nationwide. It was the era of the Beatles; rock music, first coming into vogue in the '50s, was maturing, and it was saturating the culture of young America. Jim was part of that culture, and it had an impact on him.

There were also particular musicians that influenced him including Ray Charles, Sonny Clark, Keith Jarrett and Edwin Hawkins.[101] These black artists would prove to be a key inspiration for Jim's composition and performance in years to come. Hawkins had released "O Happy Day" as a single in 1967, and an album by the same title in 1969 (a Grammy award winner). That included additional songs such as Hawkins' arrangements of, "I Heard the Voice of Jesus Say," "Jesus Lover of My Soul," and "To My Father's House." Jim says that when he first listened to the Hawkins album, he loved it and knew that was where he wanted to go musically.

Since the Covenant College music program at the time wasn't geared to country music, jazz, rhythm, black gospel, blues or rock, Jim had to do something extracurricular. He organized the "Black and Blues Band," vocalists and instrumentalists who were fellow students. The group would perform Edwin Hawkins numbers and similar music, sometimes for students, often for church congregations, and occasionally just for the fun of it. This didn't earn credits for graduation, but it was immensely popular with the student body and alumni of the college. It also provided a vehicle for exploration of a different musical world.

---

[101] *James Ward, Facebook.* https://www.facebook.com/pg/jamesward_music/about/ (accessed September 18, 2017).

Third Street Sunday School

There was a tiny "world" waiting for Jim not far from Covenant, at the foot of Lookout Mountain. In early 1971 Jim and his fiancée, Beth Moore, began to attend Third Street Sunday School.[102] Beth's father was the principal of the private school she attended in Hopewell, Virginia. He had been criticized by some of the parents because he made it known in 1962 that he would never deny admission to a student simply because he or she was black. Beth also sat under the preaching of Kennedy Smartt,[103] and recalls that every time he talked about sin, he talked about racism. Both Jim and Beth had become convicted that their predominately white church needed to do more than it was doing to reach out to the African-American community.

Third Street Sunday School, small as it was, provided an opportunity to do just that, to put out a "welcome mat" to the community through music. A new kind of worship music was needed. Within three months after first attending Third Street, Jim had dashed off the upbeat "Morning Sun," first sung on April 11, 1971, at an outdoor Easter service:

Morning Sun[104]

Verse 1

On the first day of the week
Mary came, the grave to seek.
Jesus met her by the way,
On that first Resurrection Day!

Chorus

---

[102] See chapter 3.

[103] It is worth noting that Kennedy Smartt had a role in the establishment of NCF, having a pivotal role both the Nabors' and the Wards' lives (see p.42).

[104] James Ward, licensed under a Creative Commons Attribution—Noncommercial 3.0 (used by permission). Also found In the Great Commission Publications *Trinity Hymnal*, second edition.

Rising like the morning sun,
Bringing hope to everyone (who sees Him),
Praise the Lord! His work was done,
Jesus is my morning sun!

Verse 2

Hiding in that secret room,
His disciples, full of gloom (and sorrow),
Suddenly, the Lord appeared,
Death is conquered! Dry your tears!

Chorus

Verse 3

Then, at last, on the mountaintop,
Angels told them, you should stop (your crying),
Jesus Christ will come again,
What a glad reunion then!

Chorus

New City Decision

In the summer of 1972, right after graduation from Covenant, Jim and Beth married at her home church in Hopewell, Virginia. Jim, now solidly committed to music as his vocation, had been invited to become the organist at a church in Pennsylvania, which he considered. But on the newlyweds' trip back from Hopewell to Chattanooga, the two had a chance to discuss their future. Jim wasn't at all sure that he wanted to commit his vocation to a pipe organ; he wanted to pursue the kind of work he was already doing at New City. So he met with Randy Nabors, who told Jim that he was greatly needed at NCF. Randy offered him the job of music director, the proposed contract for which was: "We'll work something out." That sounded definitive enough to Jim, and he accepted the offer.

In addition to his position at New City, Jim was invited by Pete Hammond, coordinator of InterVarsity Christian Fellowship in the Southeastern U.S., to tour college campuses, with InterVarsity sponsoring solo concerts. Ultimately Jim was hired as a campus intern for the organization and performed at its Urbana, Illinois convention in 1974. The InterVarsity connection consumed a whole lot of miles on the road. It was during this time that Jim composed "Highway,"[105] released in 1979 as part of his *Mourning to Dancing* album.[106]

So it was that Jim's continuing interest in concert performances and recording paralleled his participation in the fledgling Inner-City Missions[107] that became New City Fellowship Chattanooga. The mission paid $185 every 2 weeks, and InterVarsity rounded out a living.

In June 1975, the Wards took what turned out to be a three-year break and moved to upstate New York. There, working with Boston musician Ed Mathews, they organized a band ("Elan") which for a time did concert tours. But eventually, as happens to so many bands, the group broke up and in summer, 1978, the Wards returned to Chattanooga. During the move, Jim composed "Gotta Get Home," also on his *Mourning to Dancing* album. When the Wards got back to Chattanooga, they decided to stay for a while. That was 40 years ago.

SCRIPTURE IN THE SONGS

Virtually all of Ward's music is Scripture-based. Very many of his lyrics are direct quotes from the Bible. One example:

---

[105] The first stanza of "Highway" captures the grind a traveling musician must endure: *"Rain is on the highway beating, we were living in the car / Still beside my wife is sleeping, can you tell me where we are / Oh, a hundred miles from the Tennessee line / No, I checked my watch and it's quarter to nine."* "Highway", words by James C. Ward, music by James C. Ward and Bob Schiff, copyright 1979, James C. Ward (used by permission).

[106] A complete listing of Ward's recordings can be accessed at http://www.jameswardmusic.com.

[107] See p.57.

Who Can Separate Us[108]

Chorus

*Who can separate us from the love of Christ
Famine, persecution, danger, or war
No, in all these things we are conquerors and more
Through the One who gave his love*

Verse 1

We know that in everything God works for the good
Of those he knew before would be his own
But as we turn to answer him, what can we say
Won't his grace continue through Christ Jesus anyway

Chorus

Verse 2

Creation groans expectantly for us to be revealed
And suffering can't compare with what will come
The Spirit helps our weakness if we wait impatiently
What the Lord will do for us is still too hard to see

Chorus

Verse 3

Your God does not intend you be a slave again to fear
But you receive his Spirit as his sons
And sons of God inherit both the glory and the pain
Serving with Christ Jesus makes the answer very plain

Who can separate us from the love of Christ?

Ward simply took this passage from Romans 8 and set it to music. This is what Handel did in composing *Messiah*. Nothing is more powerful than Scripture set to music. Jim had not only learned but also experienced that when he was growing up with psalmody. Scripture and music are both in his bloodstream. As

---

[108] "Who Can Separate Us," words and music by James C. Ward, copyright 1979, Music Anno Domini (used by permission).

zealous evangelists and committed ministry professionals, Sam and Rosalie had also enrolled their children in Bible memorization programs, which Jim participated in from elementary school through eighth grade. When Sam and Rosalie Ward had their six children sit down to sing around the table using the *Bible Songs Hymnal*, an old-fashioned psalter, they were giving their children an incredible gift. When singing is melded to Scripture, it touches something deep inside the believer—something that can't be adequately put into words.

Jim Ward has done for the church what his parents did for him. He has Christians singing the Bible. It might have been St. Augustine, or Martin Luther, or someone else, but *somebody* said, "He who sings, prays twice." When Christians sing the truths of Scripture, they worship with the mind and heart, with the brain and spirit. For this reason, worship music is commanded throughout the Bible. Nowhere is that more explicit than in 2 Chronicles where the Lord, through King Hezekiah and the prophets, not only commanded music in temple worship, but even specified the kinds of instruments to be used, and who should play them.[109] Music is not just an adornment of worship, nor is it merely an option. It is essential, mandated by God himself. It's also something Christians love to participate in, and it claims a supremely high place in the Christian's life—indeed, so high a place that Jesus sang with his disciples as the Last Supper drew to a close: *"And when they had sung a hymn, they went out to the Mount of Olives"* (Mt. 26:30).

Some have wondered what that hymn was. It had words; it had a tune. Possibly it was a Psalm. But within just a few days, and forever after, Jesus' disciples would be singing hymns like "Death Is Ended," a choral piece Jim composed in 1982.

---

[109] "And [Hezekiah] stationed the Levites in the house of the Lord with cymbals, harps, and lyres, according to the commandment of David and of Gad the king's seer and of Nathan the prophet, for the commandment was from the Lord through his prophets. The Levites stood with the instruments of David, and the priests with the trumpets." (2 Chron. 29:25-26).

Death Is Ended

It was in May of 1982 that Jim's younger brother Timothy had died of leukemia. In November a member of New City Chattanooga, Marie Jennings, died. NCF's choir director at the time, Bryan Holland,[110] asked Jim to compose a piece testifying to the hope of the resurrection. "Death Is Ended" not only fulfilled Holland's request, but served as Ward's own testimony as to the peace that was his because of the promise of the resurrection.

"Death Is Ended" has become almost required music at Easter services and funerals in the New City family. The lyrics are taken from 1 Cor. 15:51-57. The score is a powerful mix of four-part choir and instrumental accompaniment made up of trumpets, keyboard, drums, cymbals and any other musical instrument on the premises. On Easter, it's typically "performed" by the choir, but quickly becomes congregational singing as retired choir members and everyone else in the sanctuary join in. Most New City congregants have learned it well, and revel in its beauty and power:

Death Is Ended[111]

Chorus

Death is ended
Death is ended
Death is swallowed up in victory

Verse 1
Behold I tell you a mystery
we will all be changed, changed
In a flash! (even in the twinkling of an eye)
at the last (the trumpet will sound)
and the dead (will be raised imperishable)

---

[110] See p.64.
[111] "Death Is Ended," words and music by James C. Ward, copyright 1982, James C. Ward (used by permission).

and we'll be changed around
The saying that is written will be true!

    Chorus

Verse 2
Our days are like the flowers of the field
The wind blows over and we're gone Gone, gone
Everlast! (but from everlasting)
Everlast! (to everlasting)
Still his love (still his love is for those who fear him)
His promises live on!
The saying that is written will be true!

    Chorus

Thanks be unto Jesus
Thanks be unto God
He has won the battle
Through the power of the cross
Where oh death (Where is your victory?)
Where oh death (Where is your sting?)
Where oh death (You are the enemy)
but Jesus is my King!
The saying that is written will be true!

Death is ended, yes!
Death is ended, yes!
Death is swallowed up in victory!

Victory, yes!
Victory, yes!
Victory, yes!
Victory!

7.

BARRY & ANN

"We're coming to St. Louis."—BARRY HENNING, MAY 1991

WHILE THE LORD, through his many servants, was growing New City Fellowship Chattanooga, we know now that he had further plans. Scripture speaks metaphorically of the "arm of the Lord," so maybe it's not improper to craft another metaphor. God had something more "up his sleeve."

Ann Filer and Barry Henning grew up in the Detroit, Michigan area. They met at the church that Barry attended, Taylor Wesleyan Methodist. Ann decided immediately, even at her young age, that this was her man, but because she wasn't yet a Christian, Barry resisted getting involved. Nevertheless, she pursued him, following him to every evangelistic service and church camp she could, and as a result, two years after they met, she came to Christ. Their romance began.

Barry and Ann were married right out of high school, in 1972. Barry enrolled in college, matriculating in the Detroit area and for a year in North Carolina, graduating in 1977 with a bachelor's degree from William Tyndale College, at that time located in Detroit. By then he was pretty much convinced that he was called to the ministry, and he enrolled at Westminster Theological Seminary in Philadelphia. He graduated with his Masters of Divinity degree in 1981.

Harvie Conn

During his Westminster years Barry connected with Harvie Conn.[112] Conn, until his death in 1999, was perhaps the most noted and influential thinker in the area of urban ministries in the Reformed evangelical world. He was a Westminster product too, having graduated from the seminary many years earlier, in 1957. That year he was ordained as a teaching elder in the Orthodox Presbyterian Church. He and his wife Dorothy subsequently served for twelve years as missionaries in Seoul, South Korea (1960-72).

In 1972 they returned to Philadelphia where Conn joined Westminster Seminary's faculty, eventually becoming the seminary's first professor of missions. When he was in war-torn Seoul, however, preaching and teaching among the city's desperate poor, he had caught a vision for the high priority that urban ministries should have in biblical missions:

> Conn began a Bible study among a community of boys [in Seoul] who begged for food and collected trash. "Blessed are the poor in the Spirit," they read together in Matthew's gospel. "What does this mean?" Conn asked in an inductive study. One boy answered, "It means being sent off to the market and returning to find your family and house gone. Now I go to bed hungry." After the Bible study, Conn recalled walking through the city wondering, "What does 'the poor' mean in the Bible? Maybe this beggar boy has a better grasp of the Gospel than I do…"[113]

---

[112] Both Barry Henning and Randy Nabors testify that Harvie Conn was one of the most influential persons in their lives and ministries. Personal interviews with Barry Henning (July 27, 2017) and Randy Nabors (August 9, 2017).

[113] Cited as an account by Mark R. Gornik of a talk given by Harvie M. Conn at Trinity Presbyterian Church, Charlottesville, Virginia, February 23, 1996.

In later years, Conn's critical interaction with liberation theologies took the reality of the poor and God's solidarity with the poor as his starting point.[114]

His position at Westminster provided Conn a platform for spreading the Korean beggar boy's "grasp of the Gospel" to others. He sought out the Philadelphia poor, as well as black leadership in the area:

> The city of Philadelphia soon became Conn's classroom. The groundwork for his involvement there was laid in 1969 by Bill Krispin and a group of African-American pastors in Philadelphia who later formed the Center for Urban Theological Studies (CUTS). Pentecostal and Baptist pastors without college degrees...turned to Krispin, a recent Westminster graduate, to help provide theological education. In turn, in 1971 they formed the Westminster Theological Ministerial Institute. On behalf of the seminary, Conn joined in the work in 1973, formally directing the institute until 1975. As the program developed, emphasizing college-level training and degree completion, CUTS was born as an independent institution, with supportive involvement by Westminster although not a leadership role.[115]

Harvie Conn's teaching and example resonated with Barry. He became thoroughly convinced of the need for racial reconciliation and ministry to the poor, and believed that these matters should be front and center in his ministry. And now, degree in hand, he was looking for a job in the pastorate where he could preach, teach and experience such a ministry.

---

[114] Gornik, Mark R. *International Bulletin of Missionary Research: The Legacy of Harvie M. Conn*, http://www.internationalbulletin.org/issues/2011-04/2011-04-212-gornik.html#_edn9 (accessed August 23, 2018).

[115] Ibid.

Move to Chattanooga

A small Orthodox Presbyterian church in Chattanooga was in need of an energetic young pastor who could roll up his sleeves and get to work. The session there heard about Barry's availability, and interviewed him. They thought he fit the bill perfectly. The congregation voted to extend a call, and Barry accepted. The Hennings moved to Tennessee in the summer of 1981, right after seminary graduation, and Barry was ordained into the Orthodox Presbyterian Church. The church was predominately white and middle-class, and Barry remained its pastor for six years.

Crisis of Faith

Barry says that he found those six years to be very hard, primarily because of an internal struggle he was having. As mentioned, his experience at Westminster had convinced him that ministry to the poor and outreach to minorities should be at the core of his pastoral efforts. But he didn't know how it was to be done, or even if it could be done, particularly if he was the one trying to do it. He understood the obligation, but just didn't see the means. He preached the obligation to his congregation, too, but saw little response and no growth. He resigned the pulpit in the summer of 1987. The church closed its doors when he left.

But across town, the Hennings could see it being done pretty well, and that interested them. At New City Fellowship Chattanooga, they saw some of the things they were looking for—focus on the poor and racial reconciliation—being doggedly pursued. And that church seemed to be thriving. How were they doing it?

Barry had already begun to find answers to his internal conflict—he calls it a "struggle of faith." In early 1986, he connected with Jack Miller, who had taught practical theology at Westminster Seminary and was by then pastor of New Life Presbyterian Church in Jenkintown, Pennsylvania (PCA). Barry had of course understood the grace of God in salvation, and had long since rejected legalism as having anything to do with salvation. But he had not yet focused on God's grace as being the sole motivation and power for obedience in the Christian's life, and, in Barry's case, for obedience in the ministry. Jack Miller helped him to see that the grace of God in salvation continues on seamlessly; it is the only path to obedience, and to effective ministry. Understanding the obligation to obey, preaching it, working at it—all these are important—but without God's grace at the center, it will only lead to frustration and disillusionment.

Miller was the right man to counsel Barry because he had experienced a similar crisis of faith. Earlier in his life, when Miller was baffled too, he had visited Spain at a site overlooking the Mediterranean Sea. There Miller "studied the promises of Scripture for three and a half months culminating in a mountaintop experience, or its seaside equivalent. He returned to America with two things on his mind: *adoption* and *revival*."[116] Miller had undergone a sea-change, and subsequently composed a "Sonship" curriculum based on the doctrines of grace set out by Paul in his letter to the Galatians. This curriculum would become a staple of Barry Henning's ministry, being (almost) a required class for every member at NCF St. Louis to this day.

First Involvement With NCF

During his time of personal uncertainty and upheaval, Barry had a friend at NCF Chattanooga, an African American named Carl Ellis. The two had attended Westminster Seminary together and connected again when Barry was pastoring the Orthodox Presbyterian church. Carl had accepted NCF's call as interim pastor in 1982 when Randy Nabors and wife Joan had left Chattanooga to pastor the Community Presbyterian Church in Nairobi, Kenya.[117]

---

[116] Van Dixhoorn, Chad B., "The Sonship Program for Revival: A Summary and Critique," *Westminster Theological Journal* 61.2 (1999), pp.227-246.
[117] *NCF, Brief History* (undated), p.4.

Carl was NCF's first black pastor and provided a link for Barry with NCF. The OP congregation began to participate in NCF workdays, where volunteers—including the Hennings—helped the Chattanooga poor who couldn't otherwise afford necessary repairs to their homes. Barry began to see how the gospel could be communicated to the poor through these acts of kindness. He also was now experiencing something he hadn't before: blacks and whites working shoulder to shoulder in these works of mercy.

The Hennings' relationship with NCF Chattanooga thus was already alive when the Orthodox Presbyterian church he had pastored closed its doors in the summer of 1987. The Henning family began to worship regularly at NCF and became deeply involved in the ministry of the church. Barry and Ann were getting some hands-on training and were beginning to see that God accomplishes his purposes in the church through grace.

Personal Lessons in Grace

The need for God's grace in the Henning household became apparent immediately. Resigning from the OP pastorate was necessary, but that meant no income. New City's priority was to hire an African-American associate, so nothing was open on that front. But the Hennings were committed to full involvement in NCF, and so Barry assisted in the pastoral ministry without pay.

But what to do for rent, food and clothing? The Hennings had four children now—Aaron, Jeremiah, Joshua and Sarah,[118] ranging from age 8 to 13—and so there were six mouths to feed. Barry reached back for an earlier skill he had acquired: paperhanging! He let it be known in the community that he could actually do this, and enough customers rang the phone so that the Henning household could scrape by. There was at least one time, however, when there were no calls. There was no income, and not enough

---

[118] Sadly, the Hennings had lost little Rachel, born on January 28, 1975; she went to be with Jesus a day later.

cash to buy groceries at the end of the week. Barry remembers collapsing to his knees, telling the Lord that they were flat-out dependent on him just to survive but that this was his business alone, and whatever the Lord wanted to do, that was fine. That day, the phone began ringing again. God hadn't forgotten; he had heard, remembered and provided. The Hennings testify now that such experiences have been pivotal in their lives.

This kind of subsistence living continued for three and a half years. The Hennings were forced to look heavenward every day, and the family's needs were always met. They testify that though it was hard, they sensed then, and know now, that the Lord was using those years to prepare them for their future ministry. It's one thing to read books on poverty, or to study the subject around a table in a seminar setting, but quite another to experience it; one thing to preach about it, another to live it.

The Hennings were experiencing God's day-by-day grace in meeting basic needs, captured in a song written by Sonnie Badu of Nigeria, and often sung at NCF St. Louis:

Eshe Oluwa

> *Chorus*
>
>> Eshe Oluwa, Eshe Baba o (*We thank you Lord, we thank you Father*)
>> Eshe Oluwa, Awadupe baba (*We thank you Lord, we are thankful Father*)

Verse 1

You gave me shelter when I have no other
You made a way when there'as no way
You turn my darkness into light
Awadupe Baba (*We are thankful Father*)

> *Chorus*

Verse 2

You put food on my table Daddy
You comfort me when I was lost
Who can be compared unto you
Awadupe Baba (*We are thankful Father*)

Chorus

ST. LOUIS DECISION

The Hennings' circumstances changed in 1990. NCF Chattanooga needed someone to preach when Randy Nabors, senior pastor, left for chaplaincy duties (Desert Storm) in December. Barry filled Randy's shoes as interim senior pastor and preached through May 1991 when Randy returned.

That spring Barry and Ann made a decision that was to alter their lives for all of his work in the pastorate to date. In composing this history, I didn't have to research what happened, because I was there.

My wife and I were visiting our son that May, then finishing his first year at Covenant College on Lookout Mountain. We were staying on the mountain and, being well acquainted with Randy and Joan Nabors, decided to attend New City on Sunday morning, partly to hear Randy preach.

As we settled into our seats, we learned that Randy would not be returning from Desert Storm for a few days. We were going to hear some other preacher. I was disappointed, but at least we could enjoy the singing. Nevertheless I selfishly began wishing we had left for St. Louis before the service so we could get home at a reasonable hour.

When it came time for the sermon, our luck went from bad to worse, or so I thought. This "boy" with a ponytail came to the pulpit. I hoped against hope that he was maybe a brand new elder or deacon rising to introduce the preacher, but no!—he told us where to turn in our Bibles, then read the text and began to preach.

Almost as soon as Barry Henning had finished reading the text, it was obvious that this pony-tailed boy could *preach*. We heard what was probably the best sermon on Romans 9 we had ever heard, and it's not an easy passage. I sat there listening and repenting of my horrible attitude. The sermon was thoroughly biblical, convicting, powerful and evangelistic. It was even Reformed!

I think I left my pew before the benediction was complete. I raced up to the front and introduced myself to the pony-tailed preacher. We exchanged names, and I said: "We need you in St. Louis." But that's not what Barry remembers. He insists that I told him that I was an elder, that the Holy Spirit had spoken to me about it during the service and had told me that I should tell this man that he must come to St. Louis. That's what Barry Henning remembers, and he took it to heart.

I have never been involved in the charismatic movement, but I now believe the Holy Spirit was interfering just a bit in our conversation. I said one thing; Barry heard another.[119] Whatever the case, God is sovereign in the building of his Church, and our exchange was Holy Spirit directed. Barry called me within about an hour and said, "We're coming to St. Louis." Period. That quick. I was dumbfounded, but thrilled. And I learned that the Lord, who once spoke through the mouth of Balaam's ass,[120] is apparently using that same technique today.

Before that Sunday morning, many in St. Louis had been praying for a breakthrough in efforts to establish a viable urban

---

[119] I do not believe I introduced myself as an "elder," as though I carried some level of ecclesiastical authority. I *know* I did not say that the Holy Spirit spoke directing me to tell Barry what he should do, because that is contrary to what I believe a Christian is authorized to do in the church today. Further, I would have considered it to be sacrilege, and it was untrue, since I had not heard the Holy Spirit speaking to me in a direct manner.

[120] Num. 22:22-30.

ministry. There were many in PCA churches in the area who were convinced that they needed to do a whole lot more in outreach to the poor and racial reconciliation, but they just didn't know how. They were convinced of this, praying for it, but where to turn?

We now had a big part of the answer, with new hope for a pastor. But as we started our trip back to St. Louis, new worries surfaced. Where was the money going to come from? Would there be enough interested people in St. Louis to put together a core group? Would any black folk be interested in listening to a white guy with a pony tail? Yet we had peace about it, believing that the Lord was the one directing events, answering prayer in a very specific way. And so, suddenly, the whole prospect became exciting!

Barry's role as interim senior pastor at NCF Chattanooga came to an end in May 1991, but St. Louis wasn't ready for him yet. Providentially, Lookout Mountain Reformed Presbyterian Church, which twenty-three years earlier had sponsored Third Street Sunday School, needed an interim pastor and hired Barry. He filled that pulpit for a year, from June of 1991 into the summer of 1992 when he, Ann and family moved to St. Louis.

Getting Ready

The intervening year provided a needed time of preparation for the St. Louis ministry. The basic vision was simple enough: establishment of another New City Fellowship, similar to NCF Chattanooga, in St. Louis. Interested people in St. Louis had been praying that this would include three things: a church, a school, and a relationship with Covenant Theological Seminary, also located in St. Louis. The seminary connection would facilitate mentoring seminary students and pastors who could focus on racial reconciliation and outreach to the poor. St. Louis had a vision; now they had the man; they needed only resources to fund the startup.

The Hennings weren't worried. They had learned through almost four years of subsistence living that the Lord always provides. In late summer, 1991, Barry came to St. Louis from Chattanooga to speak at an event organized by Warren Harper and some others, billed "Gospel in the Park." Warren was an African American, interested in the new ministry, who put together a musical group—a black and white band—to lead singing. The event was held at a pavilion in Tower Grove Park in St. Louis; something like forty people attended on short notice. Barry presented his vision for establishment of New City in St. Louis. Then, in early fall, Barry and Ann came again to attend a fundraising dinner held at a Chinese restaurant on Delmar. Only about thirty people showed up, but, wonderfully, about $20,000 was raised that evening to help with necessary travel, moving and other expenses involved in the transition.

Leaving Chattanooga wasn't all that easy for the Hennings, especially for Ann. The family had developed deep friendships in the Chattanooga community, and by comparison St. Louis seemed like a foreign country. But a frontier spirit was there as well, and though there was pain in the parting, there was excitement anticipating what could happen in St. Louis. And no one could have predicted what the Lord was planning to do.

8.

NEW CITY FELLOWSHIP, ST. LOUIS

*"They preached the gospel in that city
and won a large number of disciples."*—ACTS 14:21 (NIV)

BARRY AND ANN HENNING kept their commitment. From May 1991 on, Barry was locked in like a laser on building a new church in St. Louis. His confidence that it could be done never waned, and that confidence inspired others to join in.

On July 8, 1992, the Henning family moved into a small house on Pennsylvania Avenue in University City, about a mile and a half from NCF St. Louis's present offices at Hodiamont and Etzel, which are located within the city limits of St. Louis. They have since moved into a house about seven blocks from the Hodiamont offices.

Many Presbyterian Church in America people in St. Louis already knew about New City Chattanooga, either by visits or by reputation, and liked what they had seen and heard. But unfortunately, that church was in Chattanooga, and commuting would be impractical. But from summer 1991 on, the news spread in St. Louis that a *new* New City Fellowship was starting up in the area. No one knew exactly where, but the vision was there and the location was secondary. Some of those who knew of the plan had attended "Gospel in the Park"; others knew from the fundraising dinner at the Chinese restaurant;[121] still others heard Barry preach at St. Louis's Memorial Presbyterian Church (PCA) in the spring of 1992. And of course word got around in many other ways.

First Worship Services

Just eleven days after the Henning family moved into their Pennsylvania Avenue home, on Sunday, July 17, 1992, New City had its first worship service. About 80 people showed up. It convened at Covenant Theological Seminary's Rayburn Chapel in Creve Coeur, where the group met for the next two weeks.

With eyes set on the inner city of St. Louis, NCF then moved to the Murphy Blair area downtown. They used an old YMCA building formerly occupied by Murphy Blair Community Church, a plant of Grace & Peace Fellowship (PCA). New City met at Murphy Blair for about three months.

Early Ministries

It wasn't a church yet—not formally—but the first "Workday," where volunteers help needy persons with home repairs, was held on August 2, the second Saturday after the first worship service. Then a month later, in early September, a tutoring program was begun, and, at roughly the same time, a ministry to single moms. So within the first two months of NCF's existence in St. Louis, three of the ministries vital to the future of the church had been initiated. Those ministries have continued to the present.

Admittedly, it might have been a bit early to begin particular ministries (at least for Presbyterians since there was not yet a governing body). But what leadership there was believed it essential that these ministries be established early on. All three were directed to the poor, to those who needed practical help in

---

[121] See p.103.

their lives. That was intentional, a matter of high priority.[122] The sails had to be set in the right direction.

There were numerous PCA folk in St. Louis who had long desired to see a greater emphasis on the church's ministry to the poor, as well as outreach to African Americans, but who were frustrated because they didn't have a mechanism either for doing it well or for sustaining it. For this reason, many were attracted to the new ministry. One couple who early on encouraged the Hennings were Gordon and Ellen Carlson, members at Grace and Peace. Gordon and Ellen lived in St. Louis City, in a poor area near NCF's present offices, and had long shown their deep concern for the needy. They were able to help NCF logistically by sharing information about target areas and by assisting in "hands-on" ministries like workdays. They also introduced NCF personnel to local people who could help, connecting workday volunteers with individuals who needed, for example, home repairs.

Covenant Seminary Participants

Several Covenant Seminary students got involved immediately. A note had been placed on the seminary's bulletin board, and since the first few worship services were in Rayburn Chapel on the seminary campus, it was easy enough to give New City a try. Two such students who came to the first service were Jeff McGee and Jim Ward. Jim is Caucasian; Jeff, African-American. Both were studying for the ministry. Each, twenty-five years later, is still at NCF St. Louis, and an integral part of the church's leadership team.

Jim was seriously into music. In 1991 he obtained his B.A. in classical guitar from Duquesne University before he came to Covenant Seminary. His "language" was blues and rock music,

---

[122] Scripture emphasizes the need for immediacy in providing assistance to the poor: "Do not withhold good from those to whom it is due, when it is in your power to do it. Do not say to your neighbor, 'Go, and come again, tomorrow I will give it'—when you have it with you." (Prov. 3:27-28).

and he was looking for a way to use his gifts in a church setting. In 1992 this narrowed his options considerably, because at that time PCA worship style throughout the country was almost uniformly traditional. By contrast however the worship style envisioned for NCF St. Louis was a perfect match for him.

Barry Henning had already contacted the seminary about the need for a music director, and Jim and Barry connected. Barry was not a little surprised that this Jim Ward bore the same first and last name as the music director at NCF Chattanooga even though they were not at all related.[123] So in more than one way, it was truly a match made in heaven because although his roles have changed from time to time, Jim met his wife Sara at NCF, and they are still at New City St. Louis in spite of a necessary eleven-year intermission.[124]

The first service on July 19, 1992, seemed somewhat chaotic to Jim. He didn't yet know what repertoire or style was needed. But he did understand that this new church, in large part, was aiming to replicate the worship style and music of NCF Chattanooga, and so he and Barry took a trip to Tennessee where the *other*, the *original*, Jim Ward gave him a crash course in New City music. After he returned, others at NCF St. Louis helped and encouraged him as well, particularly in black music: Darwin and Lori White, Suzanne Bates, Julia Richer and Jerome Merrit. All musically gifted, they became Jim's musical and spiritual family for nine years.

But Jim's interest in NCF has not been only, nor even primarily, music. He admits to having little appreciation for the church's need to address racial reconciliation and outreach to the poor be-

---

[123] See chapter 6, "The Songmaker."

[124] After graduating from seminary in 1996, Jim and Sara continued to worship at NCF for five years. They then departed to Pennsylvania (2001) where Jim was youth pastor in a church, then served a term as missionaries to Peru for six years, returning to St. Louis in 2012. Jim and Sara received support in their Peru mission work from NCFSTL. He is now on staff at New City St. Louis and, in addition to his responsibilities as director of worship, leads the Latino outreach and serves on the pastoral staff.

fore his tenure at New City St. Louis, but that changed quickly. He was one of those who participated in the first workday on August 2, 1992, and it was all new to him. On that day, the team worked on a house owned by a Christan woman named Deborah Davis. When they finished the day's work, Deborah asked if she could come along with them on the next workday. Jim says that after that experience he began to understand what Barry Henning had told the workers before they got started: "This isn't rocket science. When Jesus saved you, he called you to love."

Jeff McGee also got involved first day out. Prior to enrolling at Covenant Seminary, he was employed in the engineering world. Although he was African-American, he had little knowledge of or interest in racial reconciliation as such. Jeff's father, when he heard of his plans to leave engineering to attend seminary, was strongly opposed. Nevertheless, confident of his calling, Jeff decided to pursue the ministry.

In 1991, prior to NCF's first service in the summer of 1992, Jeff and Barry Henning met for dinner, arranged by Leona Steele, on staff at PCA's Mission to North America. Barry asked him if he'd be willing to work with him as pastoral intern, assuming the new church opened its doors. Jeff momentarily wondered about Barry's pony-tail, but the two talked, and by the end of the evening Jeff said he would be willing. The church did open its doors, and Jeff became pastoral intern, doing a share of the preaching until personal issues caused his resignation from the pastorate in 2010.[125] He did not, however, leave New City but continued as a member of the session, in prison ministry and teaching. He is now married to the former Jo Harvey, also a long-time member of NCF St. Louis.

---

[125] Jeff's resignation was voluntary, and he regained clergy status in 2018, by action of Missouri Presbytery.

Other "First Dayers"

There were many others who were involved from the get-go, attending the worship service on July 2, 1992, including Joseph and Elfi Muutuki,[126] and Bryan and Kim Swedlund.

The Swedlunds were instantly "hooked." Both have been deeply involved ever since that first day. Among other responsibilities, Kim has become the ministry leader of Health Connection, a Restore St. Louis[127] work that connects immigrants and the poor with medical care. Bryan, since 2014, has been laboring in NCF's administrative office, doing bookkeeping as a member of the accounting team. The Swedlunds have 12 children—five biological, seven adopted.

When a Christian couple adopts, it can become a ministry in and of itself. The whole family—including any existing children—opens up to the world. Years ago, Kim had been working with Willa Merrit[128] in the "New Hope Moms" ministry at NCF. Missouri Division of Children & Family Services (DCFS) had referred to them a woman who couldn't handle her four-year-old son Gus. Kim and Willa befriended them, inviting them to family parties and events, but one day the woman called Kim and said she was "done'; she was leaving right then to go drop off Gus at DCFS. Kim fairly shouted into the phone: "No! Don't do that! Just give us a minute to think."

Kim called Brian to ask him what she should do. Brian said, "Go get him!" She did. Gus's mom brought Gus and a bag of clothing out to Kim's car and shoved in both the boy and his bag. When the Swedlunds' son Bradlee got home from school, he asked his mother what was going on.

"This is Gus," Kim told him. "You can play with him, can't you?" and they did.

---
[126] See pp.140ff.

[127] See p.135.

[128] Willa was married to Jerome Merrit, both African-American. The two helped enormously in the establishment and early years of New City St. Louis. Willa died in 2002.

Soon Brian came home from work. As he approached the house, Gus, perhaps rushing things a bit, said, "There's Dad!"

"Well, he's not *your* dad," Bradlee responded.

"He is now," answered Gus.[129]

Little Gus proved to be right. The Swedlunds were able to obtain guardianship of him, eventually fostering and then adopting him *and* six other children.[130]

The Bob and Jan Nienhuis family attended the first day too. They were formerly members at Memorial Presbyterian Church in St. Louis, where Bob was an elder. They sensed on that first day that NCF was where they belonged. Their home was in west St. Louis City, and Jan recalls many days when a needy person would knock at the door, asking for money. "We don't give money," she would answer, "but I'll fix you a meal." Often the person would accept the offer, and during lunch she'd tell them about their church. "New City," Jan says, "is a place I felt good about inviting needy persons to, because they'd be welcome. I knew they would feel comfortable."

The Nienhuises feel comfortable there too. They have six children, three biological and three adopted African-American children. Bob and Jan are continually amazed at the large number of families with adopted children at NCF. Most of these families are racially mixed just like theirs. NCF has become a place where such families can feel completely "normal."

Jim and Sara Drexler and their four children came that first Sunday morning as well. They pitched in immediately and wholeheartedly—Jim as an elder[131] and Sara as a deaconess. Sara

---

[129] The Psalmist wrote: "A father to the fatherless, a defender of widows... God sets the lonely in families..." (Psa. 68:5-6 NIV). (emphasis added)

[130] Personal interview of Brian and Kim Swedlund by Vera Parkin. September 7, 2017.

[131] Jim joined the session as a teaching elder. He was ordained by Missouri Presbytery (PCA) in 1986, having obtained his Master's of Divinity at Covenant Theological Seminary in 1984. He also obtained his M.Ed. degree from

also sat on the board of Freedom School.[132] Both had graduated from Covenant College in 1979, and together they worked at Westminster Christian Academy in St. Louis. They continued as members and leaders at NCF St. Louis until the summer of 2004 when Jim accepted an offer from Covenant College in Tennessee as dean of the Graduate School of Education.

New City St. Louis was a turning point in their lives—particularly the Sunday evening Sonship course. Thus it's no surprise that when the Drexlers moved to Chattanooga in 2004, they transferred their membership to New City Chattanooga, which they have attended ever since.

The Parkers

Mike and Jodi Parker missed the first service on July 2, but made the next on July 9. Together with their two children they joined NCF that very day, and have continued as part of New City's St. Louis ministry ever since.

Mike, born in Oklahoma, came to know the Lord at a Billy Graham Crusade in 1957 when he was just twelve years old. By that time his family had moved from Oklahoma to the Chicago area where the Parkers attended Wheaton Bible Church. After graduating high school, Mike enrolled in The King's College, then located in New York. He graduated from King's in 1968 with a degree in philosophy and believed he was being called to the pastorate. After reviewing the seminary landscape, he decided on Covenant in St. Louis and enrolled in the fall.

Jodi Todd was raised in West Danby in Upstate New York, and became a Christian at a Baptist church there as a child. A profound early influence on her was her mother Janice, a registered nurse, who had finished her career working in public health, mostly with the African-American population of "Color-

---

University of Missouri (1989) and his Ph.D in education from St. Louis University (2000).

[132] See p.133.

town," a community on the outskirts of Ithaca. Janice's loving interaction with the residents there had an enormous impact on Jodi's life.

After high school Jodi also enrolled at The King's College, where four years later she graduated with a degree in education. She met Mike there, too, and they married in 1969, just as Mike was completing his first year at Covenant Seminary.

Mike graduated from Covenant in 1972 and worked as an assistant pastor for three years in New Jersey. In 1975 he and Jodi returned to St. Louis, accepting a call as one of three pastors at Grace & Peace Fellowship, which led to Mike's venturing a G&P church plant, Fellowship of the Lamb. This continued through 1987, when Mike accepted a faculty position at Westminster Christian Academy. For 14 years he remained in that position. NCF then recruited him as associate pastor.

Jodi, meanwhile, had joined the NCF staff as church administrator in 1994. But her heart was drawn to mercy ministry, and when Tony Thompkins[133] assumed the duties of administrator, she devoted herself to diaconal work full time. Jodi displayed a sense of service to those who need help, and it was always from the heart, never merely a matter of duty.

Ashby Road

By November 1992, four months after NCF's first service, attendance had increased substantially, and the Murphy Blair YMCA was no longer adequate. A church building on Ashby Road in north St. Louis County became available, and for the next six months, into May of 1993, NCF met there. The church didn't yet have a session, but an "executive leadership team" was formed temporarily to make corporate decisions and direct the operations and ministries. They realized that the Ashby building wasn't suitable for the long term, and they began to explore the urban area for an alternative.

---

[133] See p.115.

82ND STREET

Two of the early and active participants in the ministry were Al and Susan Johnson. Al, an attorney, had attended Covenant Seminary and had been involved for years in inner-city work. He heard of property that might suit NCF's needs on 82nd Street in University City, which abuts St. Louis City proper. It was owned by the St. Louis Diocese of the Roman Catholic Church, used as St. Joseph's Institute for the Deaf. St. Joseph's was moving west to Chesterfield, a fairly distant suburb. The property was available for rent or sale, and the Diocese strongly preferred that it be put into the hands of those who would continue a Christian ministry on the property.

Al made the necessary connections, and members of the executive leadership team looked it over. They decided it would be adequate and then some. Besides a large multi-purpose room that could be used as a sanctuary, it had classrooms, an auditorium, dorms, offices and other features perfect for many of the ministries envisioned for NCF. Arrangements were made to rent the facility, and NCF continued to lease the property for seven years, through the middle of 2000.

PARTICULARIZATION

Leadership began to jell during 1993-94, leadership that would later be the nucleus of the session and diaconate. PCA elders who were regular attendees, already heavily involved, were Bob Nienhuis, Joseph Muutuki, David Mastin, Jim Drexler and Dan Wachsmuth; deacons were Bryan Swedlund and Al Johnson.

There were sufficient elders by early fall 1994 to form a session, and in a joyful service convened by Missouri Presbytery at Grace & Peace, NCF was "particularized."[134] Thus New City St. Louis moved from being a "mission church" to being self-governing and completely self-supporting.

---

[134] See p.64, ftn.70.

Tony & Julie Thompkins

For nearly 23 years, Tony Thompkins has been in New City's employ. By anyone's standards, he has proved to be a mainstay of the work. His business, financial and administrative acumen has been invaluable for a ministry that can have a tendency to veer toward the chaotic. Tony has had to learn how to capture the "good chaos," separate it from the bad, and move forward with focused energy.

Tony married wife Julie during his senior year (1995) at Truman State University in Kirksville, Missouri. The newlyweds weren't connected with NCF yet, but Tony was already aware of the church through his friends Todd Parker and Sean Degler, fellow-students at Truman State and members of Campus Christian Fellowship. Looking for employment, he came to St. Louis and began to interview in the corporate world.

Tony wasn't yet in a spot to spend money on a motel room, so Todd Parker arranged for lodging at the home of his parents. Mike and Jodi Parker, having already become a part of NCF and first-hand witnesses to its often haphazard style, urged Tony to look into helping out at the new church. *Please!* So Tony took off the business suit he had chosen for his corporate interview, replaced it with casual garb, traipsed over to the New City office (just 7 blocks) and met with Barry Henning. Barry asked him, "What do you think of chaos?" and Tony answered: "I think *controlled* chaos can be OK." Just the man. He was offered a position as business manager and has been so employed ever since.

On Tony's first Sunday—his first time ever at a Presbyterian church—he heard his new boss Barry announce from the pulpit that NCF had not had sufficient funds to cover that week's salaries, but not to worry because that morning someone had already come forward with a check to meet the shortfall. Tony testifies that he has since seen the Lord's miraculous intervention, especially in supplying money to meet NCF's obligations, hundreds of times during his twenty-three-year tenure there. He likely wouldn't have witnessed God's provision in such spectacular ways had he pursued corporate employment in 1996. "God has taught me how to balance the checkbook, both NCF's and the Thompkins'."

Tony is biracial. He and Julie have two biological children and one adopted. They feel comfortable at New City. More important to them, though, is the church's preaching and teaching, always affirming God's grace. They were fairly overcome by what they learned in Sonship.[135] Through Tony, grace has invaded the American business model at New City. Tony puts it this way:

> The ministry and mission of New City Fellowship is clear: to live out the gospel in our daily lives, to seek to serve him by loving the people God puts in front of us, and to look outside ourselves and to the needs of others first. When God lays it on our hearts to start a ministry and it's consistent with this mission, there's no question that God will provide and be faithful. I love telling the church's bankers, "This ministry is caught up in the flow of God's justice and mercy. We're not creating this budget. Rather, God is leading this, and we can trust Him to provide. Our cash flow may be weak—but look back at all He's provided." Those bankers hear about the provision of the Lord, not our cleverness or superb infrastructure. We've always acted in direct connection to the needs of the people we serve. The needs of the people far outweigh even our many present ministries. Why would we let our inadequacies stop the momentum of God's goodness?"[136]

THE BADENOCHS

Lester and Sally Badenoch both got their undergraduate degrees from Covenant College, and, as very many Covenant alumni do, took up permanent residence in Chattanooga following

---

[135] See p.97.

[136] Personal interview of Tony Thompkins by Vera Parkin. August 31, 2017.

graduation in the mid 1980s. They were members of NCF Chattanooga; the gospel within the context of racial reconciliation and outreach to the poor was exactly what they had been seeking. They wanted to be "hands-on." They also dreamed about being part of a church plant if New City Chattanooga ever sponsored one.[137]

When Barry and Ann Henning moved to St. Louis in 1992, the Badenochs' hearts moved with them, but not their bodies. They had wanted to be a part of NCF's core group in St. Louis, but the timing wasn't right: they couldn't make the move until 1996. When they arrived in St. Louis, though, they didn't need much time to adjust, because they already knew the Hennings and had been deeply engaged in mercy ministries in Chattanooga.

However, one aspect of NCF St. Louis markedly different from NCF Chattanooga was outreach to immigrants.[138] St. Louis, for a variety of reasons, has become a favorite American destination for immigrants from around the world. Lester's background was in construction, and apartments near the church office on Hodiamont needed repair and remodeling to make them more "immigrant friendly." Lester provided the know-how and much of the labor. For more than 20 years, Lester has been fully engaged in construction and related work under Restore St. Louis, where he serves as director of training for the Harambee ministry.[139]

Sally and Lester have six children, all of whom have been raised in the NCF world. It is what Christian parents want, and

---

[137] New City Chattanooga did in fact plant a new church, New City East Lake, but many years after the Badenochs moved to St. Louis. See p.74.
[138] See p.121.
[139] See p.134.

few obtain: to have their kids *experience* mercy ministries while hearing the consistent preaching of the gospel.[140]

THE CHAPPEAUS

In May 1993 Gerry and Sharie Chappeau came into the ministry. For many years they had been members of Maplewood Bible Chapel, a church in the Plymouth Brethren tradition; Sharie's mother and father were longtime members there, and it was where Sharie was raised.

In 1957 Maplewood Bible helped sponsor a summer Bible camp for its youngsters, including Sharie, aged 8. One night she heard the camp speaker retell Jesus' Parable of the Lost Sheep.[141] Sharie identified with the lost lamb more than with the 99 who were safe, and as she went back to her cabin, she realized that she wanted to be found. She wanted to become a Christian more than anything in the world but didn't know how. So she woke her counselor, who explained the way of salvation to her, and that night, in the wee hours, Sharie believed.

Gerry was raised in the Missouri Synod Lutheran Church and went to a Lutheran school. His mother was a believer; his dad a "lapsed" Catholic. In March 1967, at an InterVarsity Christian Fellowship meeting at the University of Missouri at Rolla, Gerry was challenged with the Lordship of Christ: "If he's not Lord *of* all, he's not Lord *at* all." Gerry came away from that conference owning the Lordship of Christ in every sphere of life—and, more personally for him, Jesus as Lord of *his* life, no matter where that might lead.

Sharie and Gerry married in 1969 and lived for a few years near the Rolla campus while Gerry worked on his graduate degree, and Sharie worked on her undergraduate. During this time they immersed themselves in befriending the hundreds of in-

---

[140] Personal interview of Lester Badenoch by Vera Parkin. September 4, 2017.
[141] Mt. 18.

ternational students at UM Rolla, mostly Indian, Muslim and Southeast Asian. They briefly considered going to India as missionaries but their efforts were providentially frustrated.

The Chappeaus returned to St. Louis after Gerry graduated; Sharie finished her degree from UM St. Louis the next fall. The two continued to be involved with InterVarsity at Washington University. They also began to raise a family, now with six children: two biological and four adopted. Three are African-American. So now they had a racially mixed family and a continuing life interest in cross-cultural evangelism.

There was something else at work, too. Both felt they had not fully experienced the God of grace in their endeavors. When they first visited New City St. Louis, they promptly met with Barry Henning, who told them of his own struggles with "works" theology, and how the bright light of grace had shone in his life.[142] The Chappeaus came away with the conviction that hard work, without a daily dependence on God's grace, would choke the life out of them. Sensing that New City demonstrated a truly biblical theology of grace, not just in theory but in practice, they joined the church.

Their ministry of choice, not surprisingly, was to work with students. Their IVCF experience at Washington University had given them one particular insight: while many students were participating in InterVarsity Bible studies, many seemed more interested in a worldly lifestyle, in making money, in establishing successful careers. Yet Washington University, located in University City, was less than a mile from the inner city. The Chappeaus wanted to bring university students into a direct relationship with the grimy streets of the society right next door.

They talked with InterVarsity about their concerns, and suggested they might set up a "spring break thing" where students from Washington University and elsewhere could come to St.

---

[142] See p.96.

Louis to personally minister to those truly in need? IVCF agreed. It began with just seven students the first go-round, but the ministry grew and was named "City Lights." The Chappeaus managed it, working with InterVarsity and New City to make it happen. Eventually, hundreds of students from around the nation (some from around the world) came each year. During the 24 years of City Lights' existence (through 2017 when the ministry was folded into Restore St. Louis's Workday program[143]) more than 5,000 students came to St. Louis to participate in the ministry.

Purchase of 82ⁿᵈ Street Property

All through the '90s, New City continued to rent the 82ⁿᵈ Street property from the Diocese, and though it fully met the needs of church and school, it belonged to someone else. Leadership and parishioners were united in their desire to purchase the complex, but the price tag (though a bargain at $1.25 million) seemed out of reach.

Moving forward with prayer, seeking the Lord's will and provision, in July 2000 the matter was placed before the congregation, and members voted to purchase the property. The session initiated a capital funds campaign, soliciting gifts and pledges. The campaign maxed out at about $450,000—almost all pledges. One third of the way there, but not nearly enough.

New City constituents, though, weren't the only ones who had a vision for the new church, or who wanted to see it permanently located on that property. The Lord has a big kingdom, means without limit, and can "make a way when there is no way." A couple from a suburban PCA church, Twin Oaks Presbyterian, decided to get involved. Wonderfully, they contributed $100,000 per month over eight months so that the purchase could become a reality.

---

[143] See p.136.

It was a done deal. New City Fellowship St. Louis now owned the whole 10 acre facility. The Body of Christ was working together in amazing ways. Not just in the purchase of the property, either: one of the donors became involved in NCF's tutoring program.

Africa Connection

It was in 1995 that the first African immigrants began to attend NCF. Early on they were from Rwanda, but more immigrants, from Uganda, Kenya and Congo, soon came along. Barry Henning and others, sensing the Lord's leading, traveled to Africa to form relationships with the immigrants' home churches and pastors. NCF pledged support to Christian orphanages and schools in Africa. Contacts were made with missionaries and pastors there to help determine the ministries most worthy of assistance—all these in lands where unemployment often tops 90%. The vision of what should and could be done in the name of Christ for these brothers and sisters was laid before the congregation, and believers at NCF gave liberally.

The St. Louis immigrants also needed help locally. America is known worldwide as a land of opportunity, but immigrant families needed help even to access those opportunities. Typically, they had little or no money. They needed assistance in finding employment, bridging the language barrier, getting enough clothing to keep warm during mid-western winters, finding medical help when needed, and myriad other essentials. NCF's ministries were defined and shaped in accordance with these basic needs.

The year 2000 saw another significant influx of African immigrants. It was also in 2000, continuing through 2005, that 82nd Street instituted four worship services: two in English in the main sanctuary and, in the auditorium, one in French for African immigrants and another in Spanish for the Hispanic population. Bill Yarborough had begun NCF's Latino ministry in 1997, and through him the church became involved in missionary work in both Peru and Colombia.

NCF's relationships with churches in Africa were continuing to develop. In 2002, NCF began formal connections with congregations in Kinshasa, Congo's capital city. This facilitated both short term mission trips to Congo by people from NCF, and trips to the United States by African pastors for additional theological education.

New City's overseas ventures have not been limited to Congo, however. Presently, similar relationships exist between NCF and London, Togo (West Africa), Lahore (Pakistan), Burma, Uganda and Zimbabwe.[144]

Congo: Tim & Kathy Rice

But when such connections are made, when needs become known, and opportunities for hands-on ministry appear, Christians should be aware that becoming seriously involved may lead to a radical life change.

That happened to Tim and Kathy Rice, who began to attend NCF St. Louis in 1994. Tim is an M.D. who was an associate professor at St. Louis University School of Medicine; Kathy is an R.N. Both, for some time, had considered how they might use their training and gifts on the mission field. Their move into the west part of the city with other NCF families was the first step in following God on such a mission.

Relocating into the city from the suburbs made it easier for Kathy to minister to the single moms in the ministry she co-founded called "New Hope Mom's Ministry." Tim headed "Health Connection," New City's medical ministry to the poor and immigrants. The Rices' one-on-one connections with Congolese Christians both in St. Louis and in Congo, together with several short-term mission trips to Africa sponsored by New City,

---

[144] *New City Fellowship St. Louis: International Missions*, http://newcity.org/universitycity/international-missions/ (accessed October 3, 2017); see also http://www.congohealthconnection.org.

provided their needed links: God gave the Rices a giant heart for Congo. They heard the call; they answered the call.

After stopping off in France for almost a year to study French, the Rices arrived on July 20, 2015 at their destination: Vanga Evangelical Hospital, something over 300 miles east of Kinshasa, Congo's capital. Tim is now head of the hospital, and Kathy is head of the nursing school. Their goal is to maintain excellent, low-cost medical care in a nation with severely limited resources. Because Vanga Evangelical is a teaching hospital, they are able to train the next generation of physicians, nurses and medical staff in "Christ-centered, whole-person care." Their long-term goal is to restore life and health not in Vanga alone, but across the Democratic Republic of the Congo as a whole.[145]

Kirk Ward

The St. Louis Jim Ward, who had been NCFSTL's director of worship from its beginning in 1992, had departed for a period of time in 2001 to pursue other ministries.[146] The church was able to make do with able local talent for a short time, but needed a full-time person to fill Jim's shoes.

The search committee apparently believed that continuity—even in the name—was important. They found that Kirk Ward, son of Chattanooga's Jim Ward, was available, interested, and highly qualified. He and his wife Sarah Meiners Ward came to St. Louis as newlyweds in 2004, and Kirk would continue as NCF's director of worship for 12 years. Kirk had received his bachelor's degree in music and jazz at the University of Tennessee. He had also been immersed in New City music from his earliest memories, being raised in Jim and Beth Ward's home in Chattanooga and attending New City Chattanooga for all his formative years.

---

[145] *Congo Health Connection: Vanga Evangelical Hospital*, https://www.mdfinstruments.com/crafting-wellness/congo-health-connetion-vanga-evangelical-hospital/ (accessed October 20, 2017).

[146] Jim returned to NCFSTL in 2012; see p.108, ftn.124.

An accomplished guitarist and composer, Kirk has developed his own style. He communicates a solid confidence in the gospel of grace without being bombastic or grandiose. His approach is thoughtful, calling his audience to reflect on the truths of scripture and own them. And just as was true for his grandfather Sam Ward and his father Jim, scripture is paramount for Kirk. Just a few of the selections on his 2009 album, *Guardian Grace*, give us a clue: "Rejoice In The Lord" (Phil. 4:4), "Jesus My Great High Priest" (Heb. 4:14), "Search Me" (Psa. 129:33), "Greater Is He Who Is In Us" (1 Jn. 4:4) and others. So like his progenitors, Kirk has Christians singing the Bible.[147]

Kirk and Sarah have five children, two biological and three adopted. They moved back to Chattanooga from St. Louis in 2016, where Kirk has 'joined the band': he's employed as the director of the instrumental music program at Chattanooga Christian School. The family, of course, attends NCF Chattanooga.

Tony and Tanya Myles

For many years the 82nd Street congregation had been hoping and praying for an African American to work with Barry Henning in pastoral work and preaching. But black leadership was difficult to find in the PCA. Probably the most significant reason is that when the PCA was formed in 1973, it was mostly a southern, white denomination. But gradually, things had been changing. NCF in St. Louis became a direct beneficiary of that change in 2008, when the congregation called Tony Myles, an African American already ordained as a teaching elder in the PCA, as associate pastor.

Tony was not raised in a Christian home. Church for Tony's St. Louis family was pretty much restricted to Christmas and Easter. But in 1992 a good friend invited him to attend the Church

---

[147] See p.90. A complete listing of Kirk's recordings can be found at ncfmusic.com and kirkwardmusic.org.

of the Holy Communion in University City (Baptist) where Tony heard the gospel preached. At age 15 Tony came to know the Lord. From that point forward, he had more than an inkling that the pastorate was in his future.

Tanya was raised in St. Louis too and grew up in the Missionary Baptist Church. She can't remember a time when she wasn't a believer, but she does remember a philosophy class she took at Southern Illinois University that raised many questions in her mind. During a 1998 vacation trip to Colorado, the claims of Christ became very real and personal to her. Late in the summer of that year she met Tony—not in St. Louis where they both lived—but in Kansas City, where the two were singing in a choir at a Baptist convention. They were married two years later, in 2000, at Missionary Baptist. That was in the middle of Tony's college years; he graduated from University of Missouri St. Louis in 2002.

After graduation, Tony's interest in the ministry became more focused. He began searching in earnest to see what seminaries in the St. Louis area might work. He was working for United Parcel Service during that time, just to keep bread on the table, and two of his co-workers told him about Covenant Seminary where each of them was happily enrolled. Tony had never heard of Covenant, but he visited the campus, applied and was admitted. He began his studies at Covenant in spring 2003.

Getting accepted is one thing; finding money for the tuition is another. Tony's UPS wages barely met the household budget as it was. But it became a family project: Tanya's mother stepped in to help and was able to pay for the first semester. Then Covenant supplied a full scholarship for the remaining five semesters. During this time Tanya enrolled at Covenant Seminary as well, in an evening program available free for spouses of seminarians. Both graduated from Covenant Seminary in 2006—Tony with his M.Div. and Tanya with her M.A.T.S.[148]

---

[148] Master of Arts, Theological Studies.

Even before Covenant Seminary, Tanya and Tony had begun to appreciate Reformed theology, particularly *sola scriptura*,[149] one of the great hallmarks of the Reformation. Tanya got Tony to listen with her to John MacArthur's sermons on the radio program "Grace to You." MacArthur, while no covenant theologian, captivated Tony and Tanya with his careful exegesis of Scripture and emphasis on grace. They also began to read the sermons and writings of Martin Lloyd Jones. While grateful for the gospel preached in the Baptist church they had attended, they began to appreciate God's covenant of grace in the New Testament as well as the Old, and the certainty of salvation.

While in seminary, Tony met Jack Howell from Norfolk, Virginia. Howell spoke at a church planting lunch in St. Louis, hosted by Covenant Seminary, and for the last two years of seminary Tony and Tanya became increasingly enthused about the prospect of involvement in a church plant. So that's the path they followed after Tony's graduation in May 2006. That path took them to Knoxville, Tennessee, where a small group of African-American families were looking to associate with the PCA. Tony was interviewed, asked to come, and went. The Myles family, now including two very young children,[150] moved to Knoxville in June 2006, undertaking the difficult task of starting a new work, United Faith Church.

In 2008 the Myles family learned that Tanya's mother, who lived in St. Louis, had been diagnosed with cancer (from which she later died). It was devastating news, and after much thought and prayer, Tony and Tanya felt it necessary to leave United Faith and move back to St. Louis, meaning that Tony needed to find a new position. James Williams, a pastor formerly with NCF St. Louis, told Tony about an opening at NCF for an associate pastor. Tony and Tanya already knew about NCF St. Louis, having attended a few times during seminary years. He met with Barry Henning

---

[149] "By Scripture alone," the doctrine that Scripture is the Christian's sole infallible rule of faith and practice.

[150] Two more children were born in 2007 and 2010.

and the session, and in due course the congregation voted to extend a call to Tony as Associate Pastor. He thought it to be a good fit, accepted the call, and began his ministry at NCF in early 2009.

Tony is a gifted preacher, and during his five years as associate pastor he shouldered nearly half the preaching. Those in the congregation who had experienced only white preaching, sat up and took notice when Tony employed practices familiar to black congregations. Occasionally when he wanted to drive home a point, he would leave the pulpit and come down into the congregation, preaching all the way. And when a line from a hymn or song was appropriate to the sermon, he often began to sing the song, with the congregation joining in.

By the end of 2017, Barry Henning had served as senior pastor for twenty-five years. He was ready to lighten his full time pastoral duties—not so much to retire, but to increase his participation in New City Network.[151] In January 2017 the congregation voted unanimously to accept Barry's decision, and to extend a call to Tony to serve in his place. Tony accepted the call and in May of that year was installed as senior pastor by Missouri Presbytery. Tony and Barry continued to share preaching duties.

New City Fellowship South

The church on 82nd Street, during the first five years of its existence, had attracted a significant number of members from the south part of St. Louis. For the next five years, through 2002, these members were praying that the Lord would open the door for the establishment of such a ministry in their area.

In the fall of 2003, with the session's approval, the "southside folks" began a separate worship service in the 82nd Street auditorium. More than 100 people attended the first Sunday. For the next year, these worship services continued on 82nd Street, with Jeff McGee and Bill Yarborough doing most of the preaching. After that year, the decision was made to move.

---

[151] New City Network is discussed in chapter 11.

On November 7, 2004, a bit more than twelve years after NCF St. Louis got its start, NCF South held its first worship service in rented space at the Chapel for the Exceptional on Winnebago Street, a couple of blocks east of Grand Avenue. The congregation would continue to meet at that location for two and a half years, and during that time it grew.

But it wasn't without difficulty and challenges; there were trials early on. One of them was that for disciplinary reasons, some of the leadership had to leave the work. But the leadership that remained and the constituency persisted, being convinced that the Lord had called them to this work, and that he would sustain them through any crisis. Barry Henning often came to preach. The NCF session[152] helped to stabilize the new work during this difficult period. The church survived and continued to grow.

Move to Grace Avenue

The location on Winnebago was nearly perfect, but the building was available only on Sunday mornings, and something permanent, available "24/7," had to be found. A church building formerly occupied by Harmony Baptist Church at 3502 Grace Avenue—a block west of Grand and only seven blocks from Chapel for the Exceptional—was available for lease, and the church moved there in June, 2007. They continued to rent the facility until they were able to purchase it in May, 2009, for just $250,000. Now New City South had a permanent, very adequate facility.

Macklann & Rose Basse

Up through March 2007, for about two and a half years, NCF South had no full-time pastor. As mentioned, Jeff McGee, Bill Yarborough, and Barry Henning participated in the preaching. Additionally, Macklann Basse, who had graduated from Cove-

---
[152] New City Fellowship on 82nd Street and New City Fellowship South are under the governance of one session, with separate worship sites.

nant Seminary in May, 2006, helped out. Macklann and his wife Rose had come to St. Louis in 2002 for Macklann's training, and during that time attended NCF. Since they were from Togo in West Africa, they found NCF's outreach to the immigrant community both attractive and important. Macklann was ordained as a teaching elder on March 3, 2007 by the Togo Presbyterian Church in a service held at NCF on 82nd Street. A pastor from Togo traveled to St. Louis for the occasion.

Macklann, the first paid staff member at NCF South, continued to assist in the preaching and pastoral ministry of the church until 2010, when he and Rose returned to Lomé, the capital of Togo, to serve as missionaries under Presbyterian Mission International, an agency headquartered at Covenant Seminary in St. Louis. There they have helped establish Africa Missions With Nations, an organization that trains "future missionaries to plant churches and disciple Africans to care for the least among them."[153]

Kevin & Stephene VandenBrink

Kevin VandenBrink was raised in Holland, Michigan, where his family attended a Christian Reformed Church. He became a Christian in 1985 while in high school and after graduating enrolled at Taylor University in Indiana. There he earned his B.A., but much more importantly he won the hand of Stephene, also a student at Taylor. They married in 1991.

Kevin wanted to get theological training after graduating from Taylor, and chose Covenant Seminary. He was much attracted to Covenant's Schaeffer Institute,[154] which, in Kevin's words, offered, "The best parts of Reformed theology, with a warm out-

---

[153] "PMI Missionaries," http://www.pmiweb.org/mb.php (accessed October 24, 2017).
[154] The Schaeffer Institute is named after the late Presbyterian theologian and author Francis A. Schaeffer, founder of L'Abri Fellowship International in Huemoz, Switzerland, https://www.covenantseminary.edu/academics/francis-schaeffer-institute/ (accessed October 28, 2017).

reach."[155] He graduated Covenant in 1994 with an M.Div. degree and by then was already working for the seminary full-time. He served there for eight years in a variety of roles, including Vice President of Enrollment and External Programs.

It was during this time that Kevin and Stephene began to attend New City on 82nd Street. They already had a vision for urban ministry; Kevin had worked at World Impact in St. Louis, an independent Christian organization ministering among the unchurched urban poor. The VandenBrinks were drawn to NCF because seeing a local church actually doing this kind of ministry as a community empowered by the gospel was exciting to them, and Kevin decided in 2002 to pursue that kind of ministry.

After about four years as an associate pastor at Green Lake Presbyterian Church in Seattle, Kevin accepted a call as senior pastor at NCF South City. He and Stephene moved back to St. Louis in April, 2007, just two months before the church moved into its permanent facility on Grace Avenue, and Kevin continued as senior pastor for 10 years.[156]

Ministry to Immigrants

A church doesn't always have to send a missionary across the waters to reach people of different races, nations and languages. One of the primary reasons for NCF South's original decision to locate in the South Grand area was that a great many immigrants and refugees had settled there, most of whom were unchurched. In 2007, refugee families from Congo and Burma began to attend NCF South, and many became members. In 2008, additional immigrant families arrived, these from Bhutan and Nepal.

These people groups grew in number at the church, such that on one Sunday morning in 2010 sixty new members were

---

[155] Personal interview with Kevin VandenBrink. October 10, 2017.

[156] In 2017 Kevin resigned the pastorate at New City South. At this writing, Roy Hubbard continues as associate pastor, as the church is searching for a new senior pastor.

received on affirmation of faith. At one point, the Nepalese population alone was more than one hundred, although many have since departed in an effort to establish a Nepalese church plant in St. Louis. But refugees and immigrants continue to stream into the neighborhood; the opportunity for witness and outreach continues unabated and appears almost endless. It's "foreign missions" right here in America.

Nevertheless, in 2008 NCF South did send out its first overseas missionary, Anna Gallant (now Anna Tuinstra), a linguist and graduate of Covenant Seminary, who works with Wycliffe Bible Translators. She is stationed in Cameroon, just east of Nigeria. Anna is helping to develop an alphabet for the Ipulo people, who have no written language, so that the Bible can be printed in their own tongue. The work is slow and tedious, but with the help of New City South, Anna is able to be out there, doing that. She is confident that the gospel must be published among all nations.[157]

Roy and Emily Hubbard

Roy Hubbard is an African American raised in New Orleans, one of five children. He became a Christian through his mother's witness and example. She took all the Hubbard children to a Missionary Baptist church where Roy responded to the gospel at an early age, believed in Jesus and was baptized.

Emily Chapman grew up in the Presbyterian Church in America. During childhood her family moved several times to different locations in Mississippi and Georgia, always finding a PCA church to attend. She cannot recall a day that she didn't know Jesus as her Savior.

Roy received his B.S. in education from Louisiana State University in 2004. While at LSU he became involved with Reformed University Fellowship,[158] holding his membership at South Ba-

---

[157] Mk. 13:10.

[158] Reformed University Fellowship (RUF) is the campus ministry of the Presbyterian Church in America. Its ordained, seminary trained campus

ton Rouge Presbyterian Church (PCA). He felt called to the ministry and in 2005 enrolled at Reformed Theological Seminary in Jackson, Mississippi, graduating with his M.Div. in 2008. During seminary Roy and Emily had married, and after graduation they began to work with RUF at Jackson State University. Roy taught briefly at Clinton Christian Academy in Clinton, Mississippi, but in 2010 he got re-involved with RUF, serving as campus minister at Alabama A&M in Huntsville through 2015.

Nevertheless, his long-term interest was the pastorate, and in January 2016 a door opened. The Hubbards—now with four children—answered a call from New City South, where Roy serves as associate pastor.[159]

RESTORE ST. LOUIS

Restore St. Louis (RSL) began formally in 2002. The session felt RSL was necessary to coordinate various New City ministries at both 82nd Street and NCF South. Its stated purpose is to, "[Connect] God's people, the church, with opportunities to manifest His love in the City of St. Louis to widows, orphans, immigrants, refugees and the poor."[160] RSL is under the oversight and authority of the NCF session. Its seven ministries are:

> *Firm Foundation.* Most children need help with their homework, and some are in particular need not only with homework but also with basic academic skills. Volunteer tutors from St. Louis area churches are pressed into service to help meet that need for kids from kindergarten through high school. Children work one-on-one with tu-

---

ministers and interns work to equip students for service in both the church and the world at large. http://ruf.org/about/campus-ministries (accessed September 17, 2018). RUF maintains 156 ministries on U.S. campuses, and 6 additional in countries outside the United States.

[159] *New City South Staff,* https://newcitysouth.org/staff/ (accessed November 9, 2017).

[160] *Restore St. Louis,* http://restorestlouis.org (accessed November 15, 2017).

tors, so strong relationships are being built. Many of the students are high-risk socially and academically. Some come from low-income, single-parent homes, for example. Others are children of recent immigrants and refugees who need help bridging culture and language gaps. As of this date, Firm Foundation ministers to approximately 30 students. With a long waiting list, capacity is limited by the number of tutors and available space to meet on Hodiamont.

Freedom School. Those who had originally prayed for the establishment of New City in St. Louis had also specifically prayed for a school in connection with the church, partly because there had been a neighborhood Christian school at Murphy Blair in downtown St. Louis called Jubilee School. That school had closed in about 1990, not long before NCF started in St. Louis, but it had demonstrated a great need in urban St. Louis for good, affordable Christian education for urban kids.

Prayers were answered when a young woman named Kim Buckey was appointed the first head of school. The 82nd Street facility had been built as a school. It had lots of classrooms, a gym, a field for athletics, a cafeteria, an auditorium, dorms—even residential space. When it opened in 1997, there were only nine children enrolled in Freedom School. Today there are about 130 students.

It has been said that it's a shame when churches use their real estate only once a week, and many do. A Christian school solves that problem because the school can use the buildings on weekdays, leaving it free most evenings and Sunday. Freedom School has grown into the buildings on 82nd Street and meshes well with the church. The gym, a multi-purpose room, is used by the church on Sundays as a sanctuary. The church uses many of the classrooms for adult, youth and children's education. The separate auditorium accommodates a French language worship service, and the cafeteria serves as a fellowship hall.

The newest head of Freedom School, Angie Yarbrough, home schooled her children and holds a master's degree in education. She's married to Michael Yarbrough, NCF's director of diaconal ministries.

Harambee Youth.[161] In 1996, NCF began to form short term work teams for city kids: jobs where they could learn a trade, develop self-discipline, confidence and teamwork. The ministry is now part of RSL, and specializes in tuck pointing, a masonry skill. Their primary focus is the West End and Hamilton Heights in the city. The ministry builds partnerships that connect resources with jobs and creates relationships with individuals, communities, businesses, churches and government agencies. This is done in the context of biblically based service to the elderly, widows, immigrants, single-parent households and the poor. In 2017, Harambee Youth completed approximately $150,000 worth of free tuck pointing.

There are now about 75 teenagers in the eight-week summer program, most of them from low to moderate income households. About a third of those will continue on during the school year. In addition to providing hands-on job training, Harambee also mentors the students in a variety of life skills, including development of educational goals, college preparation, sexual abstinence and marriage, personal finances and tax preparation, composition of resumés and preparation for job interviews, vehicle ownership and operation, conflict resolution and dealing with authority. And all of the young trainees are challenged with the gospel call on their life. Many have come

---

[161] "Harambee" is a Swahili word meaning "let's pull together!"

to know Christ as a result of the relationships formed in this program.

Health Connection. Jesus sent his twelve disciples out "to proclaim the kingdom of God and to heal the sick."[162] Nobody at NCF claims the credentials of the Apostles, but it is obvious that the poor, the immigrant, the elderly and the homeless in our society are too often marginalized in the area of health care. Health Connection seeks to become an advocate for them, by connecting them with resources, improving their health literacy, and even directly providing some basic health services. With Kim Swedlund as its head, it ministers to about twenty families at any given time.

InsideOUT Prison Ministry. InsideOUT is a ministry of Restore St. Louis currently planting a church inside the St. Louis County jail. It also connects new converts with the broader church outside in order to help them transition back to freedom as vibrant disciples of Jesus within local church bodies.

This work is not just theoretical. Taylor Bruce, a St. Louis area native and 2017 graduate of Covenant Seminary, directs the ministry. He sees jail as an opportunity for inmates to experience the Lord's meeting them in the midst of their brokenness and bringing the light of the gospel into an otherwise very dark place. His teams' hope is that preaching the good news of God's kingdom reign over their lives will bring reconciliation between the inmates, their families, the broader church and society as a whole. To that end Taylor assembles volunteers to provide in-prison Bible studies and counseling. Inmates are encouraged to share Christ with other inmates as well as with correctional officers. InsideOut also trains and equips the church on the outside to enter into com-

---
[162] Lk. 9:2.

mitted relationships with inmates through letter-writing and mentorship.

The teams recognize the need for follow-up after inmates have served their sentences because society is often apprehensive about their re-entry. Instant freedom without direction and support can lead them right back into old patterns and often back to jail. Relationships with Christians on the outside help these former inmates navigate obstacles facing them on the outside.

Workday and City Lights.[163] Workday is a charter ministry of NCF St. Louis, starting up on that first Saturday in July 1992.[164] Since Workday at NCF Chattanooga had been a significant link in the Hennings' early involvement in NCF there,[165] it's not surprising that they would smuggle it into St. Louis. Volunteers from NCF and other congregations in St. Louis assemble on Saturdays, armed with hammers, saws and screwdrivers to assist people who can't afford needed repairs to their homes.

For many years students from around the country have visited St. Louis under the ministry of City Lights[166] to do the same kind of work, not just on Saturdays but Monday through Friday as well. Workday, directed by Andrew Stern, has proven to be a powerful way not only to communicate the gospel by demonstrating real mercy and servanthood to those it helps, but also to provide an opportunity for volunteers to experience the joy of the gospel in practice.

---

[163] In 2018 City Lights merged with Workday (see p.120).
[164] See p.106.
[165] See p.98.
[166] See pp.119ff.

Umetulisha.[167] The United States is possibly the best-fed nation in the world, and yet according to one estimate at least 12 million children in America don't have enough to eat.[168] NCF did not have the resources to make much of a dent in that figure, but members wanted to obey Scripture, where the Lord rhetorically asks his people, "Is not this the fast that I choose?...to share your bread with the hungry?"[169] Jesus assured his disciples, "As you did it to one of the least of these my brothers, you did it to me."[170]

Tom Shuman heads Umetulisha. With school kids as primary recipients, it provides more than 200,000 meals annually. This includes all those in the tutoring program, the kids in Harambee, and summer teams of high school and college students.

New Covenant Legal Services. It's expensive for anyone to hire a lawyer when the need arises. It can be prohibitively so when you're poor. New Covenant Legal Services seeks to fill that need. While not directly under the jurisdiction of RSL, NCLS receives some funding from them and works in partnership with New City to provide legal help for those in need.

Al Johnson, a member of NCF St. Louis, is the lawyer who directs the ministry. A former prosecutor in St. Louis County and then a private practitioner for many years, Al left the traditional law practice with a personal commitment to be obedient to what the Lord commands: "I, the LORD, command you to do what is just and right.

---

[167] "Umetulisha" is a Swahili word meaning "You have fed us." (NCF South calls the ministry "Christian Friends of New Americans").

[168] Executive Summary, *Feeding America Report*, http://www.feedingamerica.org/research/hunger-in-america/hia-2014-executive-summary.pdf (accessed February 13, 2018).

[169] Isa. 58:6-7. See Kragnes calligraphy, back cover.

[170] Mt. 25:31-40.

Protect the person who is being cheated from the one who is cheating him. Do not mistreat or oppress aliens, orphans, or widows."[171]

St. Louis has an ample supply of aliens, orphans, widows and other defenseless poor who need representation in court. NCLS has represented needy individuals who are charged astronomical interest rates on loans, or sued for rent where the living space is legally uninhabitable, or being abused by insurance companies who refuse to pay legitimate claims, and a host of other cases where the poor are taken advantage of.

Al Johnson's enthusiastic commitment to this work has brought happy relief to many of the oppressed and provides a living example of what the Lord will do through a person who takes his commands seriously.

Steve & Lisa St. Pierre

Restore St. Louis, then, charged with the administration of its several ministries, could easily become an administrative and financial nightmare; as of 2017, its budget exceeded $3 million annually. But the Master Recruiter had prepared a director: Steve St. Pierre.

Steve's family lived in Edwardsville, Illinois, and upon graduation from high school he enrolled at the University of Texas. During summer break, back in Edwardsville, he met Lisa, and she followed him to U of Texas. They both moved back to Edwardsville in 1987. Steve was a Christian, and they began to attend Center Grove Presbyterian Church in Edwardsville (PCA), where Lisa became a believer. They were married at Center Grove in 1989 and remained there for 18 years.

After graduation from Texas, Steve had borrowed $10,000 from his dad so that he and Lisa could establish a toy store in

---
[171] Jer. 22:3 (GNT).

Edwardsville. With Steve's enthusiasm and business acumen, it was more than successful. He and Lisa worked side by side in the business, and they made enough money to buy a large home in the Edwardsville area, complete with a swimming pool and volleyball courts. It was the American dream. They used it for the Lord, too, hosting weekly Bible studies for students from nearby University of Southern Illinois at Edwardsville.

One of those students, Melissa, kept pestering them with the question, "You've taught us all about our sin and God's grace, but how does it become real? What's so good about this 'Good News'?" Steve tried to explain but was personally in inner turmoil because he couldn't give a satisfactory answer, not even one that would was satisfactory for him.

One evening in 2003 as he was driving from Illinois to St. Louis, he just pulled over onto the shoulder and shouted at the Lord: "Jesus, I want to *love* you; I want to be *authentic!*" After that night, this became his incessant prayer, and he scoured Scripture for an answer. In Isaiah 1:17 he found it: "Seek justice, correct oppression; bring justice to the fatherless, plead the widow's cause." Steve knew immediately, "*that's* the difference Jesus should make in my life!"

One Sunday morning, Mark Bolyard, who had participated in NCF's workdays, told Steve about NCF St. Louis, about its emphasis on ministry to the poor, the oppressed, the marginalized. But he warned Steve: "If you attend a service there, you'll never leave!" Steve jumped into his truck, drove across the river, and walked into NCF's morning service. It wasn't even a close call; he knew instantly that NCF was where he and Lisa belonged. He called her and told her so. Next Lord's Day, she was there with him.

They're still there, fifteen years later. They sold the toy store and the big house and moved into the city. No pool, no volleyball courts, but a home where they can be directly, daily, engaged with the needy. They immersed themselves in NCF's ministry. Both came on staff in 2006: Lisa as administrative assistant to the pastor and Steve as director of RSL.[172] Isaiah 1:17 transformed their lives.

New City Fellowship Nairobi: The Muutukis

Scripture says that the Lord *devises* ways of calling people to himself, of saving them, of giving them life.[173] He can use anything—even nosebleeds, as he did in Joseph Muutuki's case.

Joseph was born in Kaningo, a village in Kitui, a province in eastern Kenya. He was not raised in a Christian home; his father was a witchdoctor who traveled around the area offering his services to anyone who wanted them. Joseph attended high school in Nairobi, Kenya's capital city. That meant living away from home because at the time Nairobi was a two-day trip by road.

Joseph had a difficult health issue while growing up: chronic nosebleeds. He sought medical help, but his doctors couldn't figure it out. He was even hospitalized for three months, but the bleeding persisted. Finally, one doctor prescribed snuff, to be inhaled through the nose, and the tobacco product gave Joseph some relief. But it was no cure, nor was Joseph thrilled at the prospect of sniffing snuff for the rest of his life, even though it was "over-the-counter."

In 1976 Joseph attended a camp in Kenya sponsored by Word of Life Fellowship.[174] A pastor there preached that if a person is sick, he should pray about it; that the Lord heals. They prayed, and Joseph told the Lord that if he would heal him, he'd serve him for the rest of his life.[175] He got up from his knees and threw

---

[172] Steve resigned as the director of RSL in 2018 but continues to participate in its ministries. Andrew Stern assumed Steve's duties as director.

[173] 2 Sam. 14:14b: "But God will not take away life, and he devises means so that the banished one will not remain an outcast."

[174] Word of Life Kenya began in 1969 when a group from Word of Life Germany came to Kenya seeking ministry opportunities.

[175] God did seem to honor such a promise by Jacob in Genesis 28.

the can of snuff into the wastebasket. His nosebleeds stopped immediately. They've not returned. And Joseph has served the Lord ever since.

Joseph also met Elfi, a German girl, at Word of Life camp. Elfi was already a Christian, having come to Kenya to work at the camp. They married in 1981, and Joseph, desiring more theological training,[176] enrolled in German Theological Seminary in 1982, graduating with his M.Div. degree four years later. He planned to return to Kenya to teach, but Dr. R. Laird Harris, late professor of Old Testament and Hebrew at Covenant Seminary, was in Europe at the time and intercepted Joseph, encouraging him to come to St. Louis, where in 1989 he graduated from Covenant with a Master's in Theology.[177]

During this time Joseph and Elfi began to attend Memorial Presbyterian Church, and were in attendance the morning that Barry Henning preached, presenting the vision for a New City Fellowship in St. Louis.[178] The Muutukis were interested, and a few months later came to NCF's first service at Covenant Seminary. The style and mission of the church were exactly what they were looking for, and the relationship has been permanent.

In 1994, the Muutukis left St. Louis and moved back to Kenya where Joseph started teaching at Daystar University, a Christian liberal arts school in Nairobi. While there, an Indian pastor challenged him to address issues surrounding race relations between Indians and Africans. Joseph says that he had departed the U.S. thinking racial reconciliation was primarily an American problem but quickly learned when he came back to Kenya that

---

[176] While in Nairobi, Joseph obtained a degree in Christian Ministry from Daystar University.

[177] Joseph also earned a master's in historical theology from St. Louis University in 1994, the year the Muutukis returned to Kenya. Much later, in 2013, he received his Ph.D in Old Testament from the University of Stellenbosch, Capetown, South Africa.

[178] Spring, 1992; see p.106.

the problem also existed elsewhere. In Nairobi, he saw the issue existing between different African tribes (44 tribes are registered with the Kenyan government), and between African and Asian residents in Kenya. Due in large part to the way he and Elfi saw racial issues being addressed at NCF St. Louis, they eventually decided to plant a New City church in Nairobi, using the same biblical principles.

New City Fellowship Nairobi began with "Pastor Joe" at the helm, and the issues existent in America are being addressed as the gospel is preached there. The congregation includes native Kenyans, Asians, Europeans, Americans, Koreans, and Africans from other nations.[179] The Muutukis testify that the original objectives of NCF Nairobi are, by God's grace, being met; that reconciliation between such diverse and divided people can happen only as we come together at the Cross. New City Fellowship Nairobi, as of this writing, has approximately 120 members.

Church Plant: Thurman Williams

In 2017 the NCF St. Louis session voted to pursue an additional church plant, aggressively setting its location deeper into the City of St. Louis. Point man for the plant is Thurman Williams.

Thurman is a "preacher's kid." His father was a United Methodist preacher in Maryland where Thurman was raised. He studied accounting at Towson State University north of Baltimore but decided to discontinue that track. In 1990 he went on staff at Young Life,[180] where he met Pete Garriott, whose son Craig was pastor at Faith Christian Fellowship (PCA) located on the east

---

[179] *History: New City Fellowship Nairobi*, http://ncfnairobi.org/wp/about/deacons/ (accessed October 3, 2017).

[180] Young Life is a parachurch ministry devoted to sharing the gospel with teenagers. It began in 1939 under the direction of James Rayburn, brother of Robert G. Rayburn, founder and first president of Covenant College and Theological Seminary. *Young Life: History*, https://www.younglife.org/About/Pages/History.aspx (accessed August 21, 2018).

side of Baltimore City in the Pen Lucy neighborhood. Thurman connected with Faith Christian, and became heavily involved in its youth and outreach ministries.

By 1994, Thurman knew that he was headed for the pastoral ministry. He enrolled part time at Chesapeake Theological Seminary in Ellicott City, Maryland, while continuing his work at Faith Christian. In 1995 he met the lovely Evie at a Good Friday service sponsored jointly by PCA churches in the Baltimore area. Evie was a member of New Song Community Church (PCA) in Baltimore's inner urban Sandtown area,[181] then co-pastored by Wy Plummer[182] and Steve Smallman.

Evie was born and raised in Columbia, Maryland, between Baltimore and Washington D.C. She had a tumultuous upbringing, but the Lord was watching over her. She became a Christian her junior year of high school, attended Penn State, and worked with Campus Crusade all through college. Evie and Thurman were married at Timonium Presbyterian Church (PCA) north of Baltimore in 1997. Wy officiated; Steve walked Evie down the aisle. Evie and Thurman continued to attend Faith.

Three years later, in 2000, Thurman got his M.Div. from Chesapeake Seminary[183] and accepted a call from New Song to serve as pastor. He continued there until 2013 when he was called as associate pastor at Grace and Peace Fellowship in St. Louis. The senior pastor at Grace & Peace, Kurt Lutjens, retired in 2017, and Thurman became interim senior pastor in January 2018 while the church undertook its pastoral search. Thus it is that the Williams family, now including 4 children, has remained

---

[181] New Song began in 1988. It is a multicultural community-based church, "worshiping God and doing justice together in Sandtown." *New Song Community Church*, https://www.facebook.com/pg/NSCChurch/about/?ref=page_internal (accessed August 21, 2018).

[182] See p.147.

[183] Thurman also earned a D.Min. from Covenant Theological Seminary in 2011.

in St. Louis and won't even need to move to begin the new NCF work.

When the Hennings moved to St. Louis in 1992, the original vision was to focus on Hamilton Heights, but the church itself wound up in University City, a few minutes west. That isn't to say that Hamilton Heights didn't remain a primary focus of the church's ministry. New City's administrative offices are in the original target area, many NCF constituents have moved there, and it's there that the church has focused its community development ministries. But many of the neighborhood residents find it difficult to trek to University City for worship, and the worship site New City has always envisioned for Hamilton Heights is acutely needed.

Thurman envisions a true parish ministry—less like NCF's University City site, more like New City South. He will focus on reaching out in an intentional way to the mostly black community in the Hamilton Heights area, attempting to build a church with local constituents, one that can infiltrate those poverty-stricken and crime-ridden city blocks with the transformational power of the gospel of Jesus Christ.

The prescient vision of those few believers who pioneered Chattanooga's Third Street Sunday School in 1968[184] continues in Hamilton Heights, now 50 years later.

---

[184] See chapter 3. Those who started Third Street Sunday School in 1968 focused their efforts specifically on the poor area surrounding the intersection of Third and Cherry Streets in Chattanooga.

9.

NEW CITY NETWORK

"And the joy of Jerusalem was heard far away."
—NEHEMIAH 12:43B

MANY CHRISTIANS TODAY, mostly in the Reformed camp, have begun to look with interest at New City's emphases, its ministries and its church plants. In the late 1980s there was just one church to look at: New City Fellowship Chattanooga. Even though that church had not yet planted a daughter church, it had experienced solid growth. It had also shown significant progress toward being cross-cultural and reaching out to the poor and to minorities with the gospel.

BIBLICAL IMITATION

Many evangelical congregations have made great efforts at cross-cultural ministry but failed. Those churches have typically had a strong vision for the work but have become frustrated because they lacked know-how. They have also been hampered if they lacked the right personnel, in particular African-American pastors and their families or others experienced in working with minorities. Such people are usually necessary to effectively interface with urban culture.

Prior to 1991, some believers in St. Louis—specifically Grace & Peace Fellowship and its daughter plant deep in the city, Murphy-Blair[185]—had braved the way and even made progress, but not as much as they had hoped for. After many of them had begun to search for new approaches, they believed that what they saw happening in Chattanooga was what they were after. So they began to pray for what amounted to a "shortcut": "Lord, please give us a New City Fellowship here!"[186]

They of course recognized that building churches is not the same as franchising Walmart stores or McDonald's restaurants. For one thing, any church planting approach will vary greatly from one community to the next. Perhaps Chattanooga was unique in being a city that would yield to NCF's approach. Maybe St. Louis wouldn't. On the other hand, why keep trying to re-invent the wheel? So they concluded that copying the Chattanooga model was worth a try. They did, and God has greatly blessed their efforts.

Imitation can be a good thing. Paul told the Corinthians to "...be imitators of me, as I am of Christ."[187] Paul also spoke approvingly of the Thessalonian believers when he wrote: "For you, brothers, became imitators of God's churches in Judea."[188] Paul was simply saying that Christians can be helped in building the church by imitating other churches. "We Thessalonians can see that those believers over in Judea are doing something right, something we want to achieve; let's copy them." Paul is not say-

---

[185] Grace & Peace Fellowship, founded in 1969 in St. Louis City, was intentionally cross-cultural, reached out to minorities and assisted the poor. The church also launched Murphy Blair Community Church and its companion Jubilee School in 1970, giving high priority to these goals (see p.73). *Grace & Peace Fellowship: Our Church History*, http://graceandpeacefellowship.org/about/our-church-history/ (accessed August 31, 2018).

[186] See p.85.

[187] 1 Cor. 11:1. The Greek word is *"mimetai,"* meaning "imitators" or "copiers." The Greek word is the root for the English "mimic."

[188] 1 Thes. 2:14 (NIV).

ing one size fits all, but just that it is good to make an effort to learn from one another.

MISSION TO NORTH AMERICA

Joan and Randy Nabors returned from Africa in 1984, and Randy re-assumed his role as senior pastor at NCF Chattanooga. Some time later, Mission to North America[189] asked Randy for help in their efforts to establish cross-cultural ministries nationwide. Though busy with his full-time pastorate, Randy agreed to help—without pay—in MNA's "Mercy Ministries." The position had been filled up to that time by Tim Keller, but Keller was preparing for an MNA plant in an area once thought impenetrable. (Redeemer Presbyterian Church in Manhattan is the result.)

The MNA board asked Randy to visit pastors and others, both inside and outside the PCA, who were specifically working in cross-cultural, mercy, and racial reconciliation ministries. Randy already knew most of them, so it wasn't new ground. He began to visit them around the country, men like Bob Becker in Fredericksburg, Virginia, who was attempting to start an NCF work there (now NCF Fredericksburg). He also talked with Mark Gordon and Stephen Smallman, both Covenant Seminary graduates who were initiating such a ministry in Baltimore's Sandtown area, New Song Community Church. There were many others, and it soon became evident that the need for effective methodology, for training, for guidance, was urgent.

ESTABLISHMENT OF THE NETWORK

By 2010, when Randy was about to step down as Senior Pastor at NCF Chattanooga, he assembled a list of the people and ministries that he had been in contact with while at MNA—people who had asked him for guidance, who were looking for a church model. Randy and Barry Henning met to brainstorm about the possibility of networking ministries and churches committed to similar goals. Both thought the idea had merit, and in 2008 they

---

[189] See p.51, ftn.49.

met with five other pastors: Carl Ellis, Wy Plummer, Thurman Williams, Jim Pickett, and Santo Garafolo (lead pastor at NCF Atlantic City), all of whom were already involved in such ministries. They decided to organize New City Network, working with but not under the authority of Mission to North America, specifically the Urban & Mercy Ministries division, headed by Randy Nabors.

So the Network was officially organized in 2010. Letters were sent to everyone known to have an interest in urban, cross-cultural ministry similar to the New City Fellowships already in existence. The response was stunning. Nabors describes it as "BOOM!" At this writing, New City Network includes the following churches, plants and ministries:[190]

Alabama
Aspire, Birmingham
Common Ground, Montgomery
Courts of Praise Christian Center, Mobile
Neighborhood Christian Center, Decatur
Redeemer Church (PCA), Jackson
Strong Tower at Washington Park, Montgomery
The Village Church, Huntsville
Trinity Gardens Church/Trinity Family Ministries, Mobile
Urban Hope Community Church, Birmingham/Fairfield

Arizona
Barrio Nuevo Phoenix, Phoenix
New City Phoenix, Phoenix

California
Bridge, San Diego
Pacific Crossroads Presbyterian Church, Los Angeles

---

[190] *New City Network: Network Directory*, https://www.thenewcitynetwork.org/network-directory.html (accessed September 4, 2018).

Soaring Oaks Presbyterian Church, Elk Grove

Canada
New City Church, Hamilton, Ontario

Connecticut
Christ Presbyterian Church in the Hill, New Haven
Grace City Church, Bridgeport

Delaware
Grace Dover, Dover

District of Columbia
Grace DC Meridian Hill, Washington
Grace DC Mosaic, Washington

Florida
City Church, Jacksonville
Hallandale Church Planting Project, Hollywood
New City Miami, Miami
NewCity Parramore Avenue, Orlando
Old Cutler Presbyterian Church, Miami
Strong Tower Lakeland, Lakeland

Georgia
New City Fellowship, Athens
Shalom City Church, Atlanta
St. Paul's Presbyterian Church, Marietta
Strong Tower Fellowship, Macon
Westside, Atlanta

Illinois
Hope Works Community Development, Woodlawn, Chicago
Living Hope Church, Chicago

Indiana
Redeemer Presbyterian Church, Indianapolis
Soma Church, Indianapolis

Kentucky
Seed to Oaks, Louisville
Sojourn Community Church, Louisville

Kenya
Kibera Reformed Presbyterian Church, Nairobi
New City Fellowship, Nairobi

Louisiana
St. Roch Community Church, New Orleans

Maryland
City of Hope Church, Columbia
Faith Christian Fellowship, Baltimore
Mosaic Community Church Silver Spring, Silver Spring
New Song Community Church, Baltimore
The Village, Baltimore

Massachusetts
Christ the King Dorchester/Boston, Dorchester
Christ the King Jamaica Plain/Roxbury, Boston

Michigan
New City Fellowship OPC, Grand Rapids
New City Midtown, Detroit

Mississippi
Christ Fellowship in Horn Lake, Horn Lake
Redeemer Church PCA, Jackson

Missouri
New City Fellowship South City, St. Louis
New City Fellowship St. Louis, St. Louis
South City Church, St. Louis

New Jersey
Calvary Gospel Church, Newark
Christian Community Presbyterian Church, Newark
Epiphany Fellowship of Camden, Camden

New City Fellowship, Atlantic City

New Mexico
Crosstown Ministries, Las Cruces

New York
Grace Church, Rochester
Queens Presbyterian Church, New York

North Carolina
Christ Central Church, Charlotte
Christ Central Durham, Durham

Ohio
Redeemer Church, Mason
Veritas Community Church, Short North Congregation, Columbus

Oklahoma
Crossover Bible Church, Tulsa
Crossover Community Impact, Tulsa

Pennsylvania
New City Fellowship of Lancaster, Lancaster

South Carolina
Living Hope Presbyterian Church, Anderson

Tennessee
Hope for the Inner City, Chattanooga
New City Fellowship, Chattanooga
New City Fellowship East Lake, Chattanooga

Texas
Christo Rey Presbyterian Church, Dallas
New City Fellowship Dallas, Dallas

United Kingdom
New City IPC, London

Virginia
Alexandria Presbyterian Church, Alexandria
Crown and Joy Presbyterian Church, Richmond
New City Fellowship Fredericksburg, Fredericksburg
Northside Church of Richmond, Richmond
Trinity/Prospect, Charlottesville

Washington
Jubilee Community Church, Seattle

Wisconsin
Friend of Sinners Church, Milwaukee

While most of these churches and ministries are within the Presbyterian Church in America, some are in other denominations and others independent.

The original leadership of NCN was chosen at the 2008 conference mentioned above. The leadership group is changed or renewed by vote of those attending its biennial conference.

New City Network is not a 'top-down' organization, but rather, a collaborative. Nabors describes it as an "affinity" association of those with common interest. It describes itself as, "A coalition of churches and ministries, urban and cross-cultural, which include the poor, which have joyful worship, and which provide sound biblical preaching."[191] It is more like a league that assists church plants as they start and develop.

As of this writing, approximately 35 church plants are associated with the network. Each of these began with local resources, often the result of the fund-raising efforts of the church planter. But NCN recognizes that outside support is needed for continuation and stability, and estimates that the typical plant will have that need for about 10 years. NCN does not directly fund the plants, but has assembled a team of seasoned urban

---
[191] *New City Network*, http://www.thenewcitynetwork.org (accessed July 24, 2017).

leaders who assist in determination of grant money to help sustain these ministries as they develop leadership and until they become self-supporting.

NCN also works with local churches in sponsoring various events throughout the year for network participants. One is the annual Reconciliation and Justice Conference, a theological and motivational conference for churches who want to pursue racial reconciliation, usually held in St. Louis. Another is NCF Chattanooga's Urban Ministry Training Week, where classes are given in the theology, ideology, and methodology of urban ministry. In the past, presenters have taught on cultural identity, development and mercy strategies, inner-city children, African-American and Latino challenges in ministry, and cross-cultural worship.

Mission to North America also offers the annual Leadership Development and Recruitment conference in late summer, bringing together current and prospective African- American pre-college, college, and seminary students for a time of fellowship, sharing, and encouragement.[192]

Randy Nabors does not describe the work of New City Network or any of its member ministries as following a "racial reconciliation," a "cross-cultural" or an "urban" model. NCN does not promote such models to the exclusion of a more important fundamental characterization: New City Fellowship is based on the gospel. While the other descriptors are indispensable to the purposes of the organization, Randy says, "If we lead with the gospel, if we really preach the gospel, reconciliation will follow."[193]

---

[192] https://www.thenewcitynetwork.org/network-events.html, accessed October 8, 2018.
[193] Personal interview with Randy and Joan Nabors. August 9, 2017.

10.

STATE OF THE CHURCH

"We and our kings, our princes and our ancestors are covered with shame, Lord, because we have sinned against you."
—DANIEL 9:8

THE PRESBYTERIAN CHURCH IN AMERICA, founded in 1973, originated in the Southern United States and was overwhelmingly white. To the founders' credit, their stated reasons for its formation were "...for the sake of the scripture, for the sake of the preservation of historic Presbyterianism, and for the furtherance of the gospel proclamation."[194] In the first years of the PCA, however, little attention was given to biblical racial reconciliation. It was not so much a matter of outright opposition as, for the most part, a profound lack of concern. Those seeing biblical racial reconciliation as a crucial part of the gospel proclamation were accepted, encouraged and even applauded from time to time, but marginalized.

Nevertheless, as Randy Nabors said, "If we really preach the gospel, reconciliation will follow." Preaching the whole counsel

---

[194] Transcript of speech given by James M. Baird, former senior pastor of First Presbyterian Church, Jackson MS, on the floor of General Assembly, June 11, 2015 (excerpt). St. Louis, MO: PCA Historical Center, http://www.pcahistory.org/topicalresources/race/2015_Baird_transcript.pdf (accessed October 23, 2018).

of God, as the PCA was committed to do and in large part was doing, has a way of catching up with you. Often this happens in ways that were unintended when the commitment was made, ways that convict not only the hearer but also the preacher, ways that can be brought about only as the Holy Spirit works by and with the Word in our hearts.[195]

The Holy Spirit had obviously been at work in the PCA. In 2015, 42 years after the PCA was formed, two teaching elders, Sean Lucas and Ligon Duncan, presented a personal resolution to the General Assembly calling for repentance for past sin in the church's attitude toward and treatment of African Americans, citing the Civil Rights movement as a particular era when the church had failed. It called on the assembly for re-commitment "…to the task of truth and reconciliation with our African-American brothers and sisters for the glory of God and the furtherance of the Gospel."[196]

When the resolution came to the floor, parliamentary procedure came into play, and the moderator stated that by assembly rules the personal resolution must be referred to a committee for further study, and meanwhile be disseminated to the PCA's 97 presbyteries. The moderator and some delegates who spoke from the floor encouraged the assembly that this might be done with the understanding that the resolution could be refined, and perhaps become an even stronger statement by the denomination, if presbyteries first approved it for consideration at the next annual General Assembly in 2016.

---

[195] "[O]ur full persuasion and assurance of the infallible truth and divine authority [of scripture], is from the inward work of the Holy Spirit bearing witness by and with the Word in our hearts." *Westminster Confession of Faith*, Ch.1, Sec.6.

[196] For the full text of the resolution, see "Personal Resolution on Civil Rights Remembrance," byFaith, Pub. June 10, 2015. http://byfaithonline.com/personal-resolution-on-civil-rights-remembrance/ (accessed October 23, 2018).

During the debate, one of those who rose to speak was Jim Baird, long-time and by then retired pastor of First Presbyterian Church of Jackson, Mississippi. He urged the assembly to suspend the rules and vote on the resolution *now*. For a pastor of a church that once spoke favorably (before his pastorate there) of racist White Citizens' Councils,[197] his confession was especially poignant:

> In 1971 twelve men were elected to form a new denomination. Take two years and form that denomination. Of those twelve men six were ministers and six were ruling elders. All have died or left the PCA except two: Kennedy Smartt and me.
>
> [Pause]
>
> And I confess, that in 1973, the only thing I understood was that we were starting a new denomination, which we did. And I confess that I did not raise a finger for civil rights. I was [tasked] with one thing, and that was to start a new denomination, for the sake of the scripture, for the sake of the preservation of historic Presbyterianism, and for the furtherance of the gospel proclamation.
>
> And so I confess my sin.
>
> I'm not confessing the sin of my fathers, I'm confessing my sin, and of those twelve men. Were we racists? No. But we did not do anything to help our black brethren.
>
> That's the first thing here.
>
> The second thing, fifty years later I'm a different man, but that's beside the point. It was my understanding that this resolution would have been passed here and would have been passed with the understanding that we confess, you men, but I confess personally that I did nothing.[198]

---

[197] See p.15, ftn.10.
[198] Excerpt, speech by James M. Baird. (See p.155, ftn.194.)

Tim LeCroy, pastor of Christ Our King Church in Columbia, Missouri, was present and remembers the response evident in the room:

> As [Baird] continued to speak and confess his, and indeed our sin, many of the men in the room began to weep. It was as if a great weight was being lifted off of us. We were finally beginning to be honest about our past and to confess it so that healing can come.
>
> I grew up Pentecostal. But that is the most intense move of the Spirit I have ever felt in my life. The presence of the Spirit was palpable as if a Holy weight was pressing down on me. Other men reported feeling goosebumps and other similar impressions. The move of the Spirit that [commissioners had] prayed for was heavily upon us.[199]

While the parliamentary snag delayed passage of the resolution, those in favor of immediate action did not yield—nor were they asked to—on the need for immediate prayer. Commissioners rose one after another, waiting in long lines to pray for personal and corporate forgiveness and transformation on the issue of race in the Presbyterian Church in America.

At the next General Assembly in June 2016 the resolution, now modified and strengthened after a year of consideration by the greater church, was presented as Overture 43 from Potomac Presbytery. After a few amendments, it reads:

Pursuing Racial Reconciliation and the Advance of the Gospel
(*Overture 43*)

Be it resolved, that the 44th General Assembly of the Presbyterian Church in America does recognize, confess,

---

[199] *Tim LeCroy—Vita pastoralis,* "The Protest of 2015." https://pastortimlecroy.com/2015/06/15/the-protest-of-2015/, p.8. (accessed October 23, 2018).

condemn and repent of corporate and historical sins, including those committed during the Civil Rights era, and continuing racial sins of ourselves and our fathers such as the segregation of worshipers by race; the exclusion of persons from Church membership on the basis of race; the exclusion of churches, or elders, from membership in the Presbyteries on the basis of race; the teaching that the Bible sanctions racial segregation and discourages inter-racial marriage; the participation in and defense of white supremacist organizations;[200] and the failure to live out the gospel imperative that "love does no wrong to a neighbor" (Romans 13:10); and

Be it further resolved, that this General Assembly does recognize, confess, condemn and repent of past failures to love brothers and sisters from minority cultures in accordance with what the Gospel requires, as well as failures to lovingly confront our brothers and sisters concerning racial sins and personal bigotry, and failing to "learn to do good, seek justice and correct oppression" (Isaiah 1:17); and

Be it further resolved, that this General Assembly praises and recommits itself to the gospel task of racial reconciliation, diligently seeking effective courses of action to further that goal, with humility, sincerity and zeal, for the glory of God and the furtherance of the Gospel; and

Be it further resolved, that the General Assembly urges the congregations and presbyteries of the Presbyterian Church in America to make this resolution known to their members in order that they may prayerfully confess their own racial sins as led by the Spirit and strive towards racial reconciliation for the advancement of the gospel, the love of Christ, and the glory of God; and

---

[200] See p.159, ftn.10.

Be it further resolved, that the 44th General Assembly call the attention of churches and presbyteries to the pastoral letter contained in Overture 55 [see below] as an example of how a presbytery might provide shepherding leadership for its churches toward racial reconciliation; and

Be it finally resolved, that the 44th General Assembly remind the churches and presbyteries of the PCA that *BCO* 31-2 and 38-1 provide potent and readily available means for dealing with ones who have sinned or continue to sin in these areas.[201]

It may have taken an extra year, but the overture was adopted by vote of 861 to 123, with 23 abstentions. For a church arising out of the segregated Old South, this seems at least remarkable.

Day of Opportunity

Thus, by God's grace and the unmistakable leading of the Holy Spirit, the church lives in a day of special opportunity, possibly unprecedented. Such a clear expression of repentance and intent for future obedience regarding racial reconciliation could not have been imagined even in 1973, less than 50 years ago. But now God has brought the PCA to this place. For New City Fellowship in particular, it's exhilarating. It is what leaders and constituents in the New City world and similar ministries had been praying for.

It is also humbling. It didn't happen because of an orchestrated plan, it wasn't a campaign, and party spirit wasn't evident. God put the pieces together. One of those pieces most evident was the tearful speech of one of the founders of the PCA. Jim Baird took the church back to its roots in his confession, thus becoming a catalyst for the transformation of the whole denomination on the issue of biblical racial reconciliation. It was alto-

---

[201] "Actions of the 44th General Assembly." St. Louis, MO: PCA Historical Center, http://pcahistory.org/ga/actions/44thGA_2016_Actions.pdf (accessed October 24, 2018).

gether the work of the Holy Spirit, and because it was his work, the church can have solid confidence for the future.

LETTER TO THE CHURCHES (*excerpt, Overture 55*)

Rightly anticipating that Overture 43 would be adopted in June 2016, churches and presbyteries around the country had already been considering its implications, how it could be implemented locally. Mississippi Valley Presbytery came to the 2016 General Assembly with "A Pastoral Letter on Racism and the Gospel,"[202] part of its Overture 55 which paralleled Overture 43. Mississippi Valley, after delineating the urgent need for biblical reconciliation in the church, recognized some of the hurdles that lay ahead:

> Most of us in the PCA churches of the Presbytery of the Mississippi Valley are white, though we live in a state with a population that is 37% black (and the Jackson metropolitan area is about 50% black). Denominationally, less than 2% of PCA pastors are black. We don't have statistics on the ethnicity of our church membership in PMV, but ethnic minorities are probably in the low single digits percentage-wise. One of the things that this means is that we will have to make a deliberate effort to gain another perspective on this issue outside of our own "bubble." Relatively few of us have close friends of other ethnicities, especially in the context of our local churches. That means that understanding the perspective of [those] who are of a different ethnicity, and with whom we have an actual relationship, on the issue of racial reconciliation, is a challenge.[203]

---

[202] "Pastoral Letter 2016, MS Valley Presbytery," St. Louis, MO: PCA Historical Center, http://www.pcahistory.org/pca/Pastoral-Letter-Overture-55-MS-Valley.pdf (accessed October 25, 2018).
[203] Ibid, p.6.

Every church, including those in the New City world, has and will continue to have such challenges. This pastoral letter sets out five suggestions for churches and individuals: learn, pray, acknowledge, relate and commit. The letter goes into some detail with regard to each.

Learn. The letter gives a list of sources for reading and audio lectures and sermons, recognizing that many Christians are woefully uninformed on race issues and the history of how the church has treated such issues.

Pray. Because the Holy Spirit has led the church thus far, and because believers know that it is only by his continuing guidance and empowerment that racial reconciliation can be accomplished, prayer is central. The letter lists specific items for praise, thanks, confession of sin, and petitions for specifics, such as breaking down barriers in the community, for God's particular blessing on minority leaders and preachers, for a sense of welcome to be present in the church for minority visitors, and for "…more African-American (and other ethnic minority) pastors, missionaries, church planters, seminary and college professors, campus ministers, elders, and deacons…in the PCA."[204]

Acknowledge. The letter calls for acknowledgment of racism as a present sin in the church, noting that this runs counter to many evangelicals who assume that urging such acknowledgment is just another attempt to foist 'political correctness' on the church; that they're tired of the discussion; that they want to move on. But the letter notes that, "Black Christians are 'tired' of having to justify the validity and relevance of the conversation in the first place and are often deeply discouraged by how little their white brothers and sisters seem to have thought or cared about it, or to have realized the dramatic effect racism has had upon their lives."[205]

---

[204] Ibid, p.10.
[205] Ibid, p.11.

Relate. The letter urges individual believers to relate, to make friends, and not to underestimate the power of friendship with those of another race. Friendships are not abstract, and they must be intentional because the natural human tendency for people of different races is to mingle with their own. And mere acquaintance is not relationship. Just shaking hands on Sunday morning is quite different from sharing a meal or taking an outing together.

Commit. Serious commitment in practical, real world ways, is essential. Pastors, elders and members need to commit the church financially: to consider establishment of minority scholarship funds for those who want Christian education and for those who want to prepare for the gospel ministry. The church needs to seek out and disciple interns from ethnic minorities for ministry. Churches should seek out qualified members of minority groups for church leadership as teachers, deacons and elders.

The General Assembly was wise to direct the church to this pastoral letter as guidance for the implementation of Overture 43. Seminary professors tell their students that no matter how masterfully they might exegete scripture, no sermon is complete without specific application: "Tell the congregation what they should do about it."

Perhaps Overture 55 from Mississippi Valley Presbytery has provided the application for the sermon contained in Overture 43.

Down the Road

So what does the future hold? No one knows specifically, but God has at least disclosed a direction. Overture 43, though just a piece of paper, signifies much more than a historical record. It is more like a map of where the Holy Spirit has been, and where he plans to go.

The church has been given an uncommon opportunity to reap benefits for the Kingdom because of changed hearts and minds in the 21st century. A door has not just been opened, but torn off its hinges. It is a time of hope and challenge: to spread the gospel of reconciliation in Christ to a nation polarized by race, social standing, political affiliation, sex, and a deluge of other issues that Satan uses to divide and conquer.

Now that the Presbyterian Church in America has, by God's grace, dislodged that door, it is important to notice that it was not an exit, but a threshold. As Winston Churchill said after an Allied victory in the Second World War, "Now this is not the end. It is not even the beginning of the end. But it is, perhaps, the end of the beginning."[206]

---

[206] "The End of the Beginning," The Churchill Society, London. Winston Churchill's address at The Lord Mayor's Luncheon, November 10, 1942. http://www.churchill-society-london.org.uk/EndoBegn.html (accessed October 24, 2018).

11.

Afterthought: Precious Stones

"Now ye are the Body of Christ, and members in particular."
—1 Corinthians 12:27 (kjv)

A GREAT THING we get from studying history, especially as Christians studying the history of the church, is to observe how we do things compared to how God does things. While what we have done is not necessarily at odds with what God has done, our ideas, plans and works are usually surprisingly *different* from his.

For example, if you attended a seminar next month advertised as *How to Establish a Cross-Cultural Ministry: A Guide for Today's Church Planter*, what would you think if you saw something like the following on the overhead screen?

1. Your plant should commence, if possible, under the auspices of a small, all-white denomination.
2. The work must not be funded.
3. Your core group, ideally, should be no more than about fifteen young African-American kids, divided into three or four smaller groups.

4. Your first meetings should be during the summer in a small apartment with no air conditioning. While their white teachers are teaching them, the children may be seated in a bathtub or the backseat of a car.

5. A flip-chart is essential for singing, led by a middle-aged white man, accompanied by a middle-aged white woman playing a portable electric organ. The songs should be traditional white hymns.

6. Weekly meetings should continue in the same small, stuffy apartment for several years. Expansion into the kitchen and hallway between the bedroom and the bathroom will accommodate any growth.

7. By about the fourth year, a part-time preacher should be hired, without compensation. He also should be middle-aged and white, hold a diploma from an Ivy League university, with primary experience lecturing at the college level. If you need someone to assist this Princeton graduate in preaching duties, it is advisable to hire someone with no education beyond a high-school diploma who has never had training in public speaking or homiletics.

Et cetera.

Does it sound like we've got a plan? Well, apparently it was God's plan. We know that for sure because it happened, and he plans everything that happens. This was his way of establishing New City Fellowship Chattanooga, eventually NCF St. Louis, New City Network, and all the rest. Is it a good list to put on the overhead at a church planting seminar? No, and yes.

No, because it looks more like how *not* to plan a cross-cultural church, or any church. But that's how it was done, even how God did it, although it would seem to be anything but a good formula. In and of itself, it doesn't list at all what we think we should be doing and probably even lists what we think we shouldn't be doing.

But we can also say *yes*, it is a good list to put on the overhead at a church planting seminar. And perhaps it should even be kept up there for a while. It may turn out to provide, as they say, a "teaching moment." If we edit each of the seven bullet points just a bit, introducing each with "In spite of the fact that we…" and tacking onto the end of each point "…this is how God established New City," we could say that this part of the seminar was most instructive. And *encouraging*. It displays in bold relief how God can use meager, often counter-intuitive means to accomplish amazing ends.

The above list of seven items is pretty much the whole inventory of what the Covenant College people on top of Lookout Mountain had available to them in 1968. Of *course* they wished that their denomination was not all white, that they had funding, that they had black leadership and all the rest. They knew they didn't have what they needed, that they were severely handicapped, but believed this work to be so crucial to the Kingdom that they had to get it started anyway.

In actuality, they did have some precious items in their "inventory": fifteen black children on the very first day. This was an enormous gift because their constituency, though all children, was exactly who they most wanted to reach. Arline Cadwell captured the essence of the theology of church planting in her recollection of Third Street Sunday School's first meeting: "We arrived in the apartment that morning, ready to sing and teach, not knowing what to expect, or if any children would attend. A few minutes after we planned to start, just as we began to wonder if anyone would come, *the Lord brought us* a little girl named Peaches Ricks."[207]

---

[207] See p.35 (emphasis added).

When you come right down to it, it's not what we have in our arsenal that's important; it's what the Lord brings us. We are on solid footing if we work with just what's in our hands. Moses knew that what he had in his hands would be utterly inadequate for freeing the Israelite nation from slavery. But God commanded him, nevertheless, to look at what he had in his hand—a stick of wood—and use it.[208] The disciples only had five loaves of bread and two fish, but Jesus told them to feed that to more than 5,000 hungry people, and everyone was filled.[209] The few who started Third Street Sunday School knew God wanted them to use the little they had in their hands on June 2, 1968, and they did. We are present witnesses to the bountiful fruit of their simple obedience.

What they did at and after that first meeting is instructive. I think it is one of the primary reasons the Lord has prospered New City Fellowship. Besides teaching the Gospel, they began to care for their little flock of followers, who at that time were only children, just lambs. They asked each of them to give their names, and Rudy Schmidt wrote them all down in a little class register. (He was well suited for this seemingly tedious job, being registrar at Covenant College.) Every week, from then on, he'd add the names of new attendees and keep track of attendance.[210] He or another leader would follow up with absentees as best they could, often going to their homes, checking to see if they were okay. It may seem a bit fussy, and it risked irritating their parents, but it sent a clear message to both the children and their parents: we care about you, not just generally, but specifically, personally, particularly. We respect you. We want you to be a part of our family, and we want to be a part of yours. We need you. Your name matters. Your attendance matters. *You* matter.

---

[208] Ex 4:2-5.

[209] Mt. 14:13-21.

[210] The original class register still exists as part of the New City Fellowship Chattanooga archives, showing attendance of each child from June 2 1968 through May 25 1969.

These same kinds of loving, caring acts of personal attention are found throughout the history of New City Fellowship. When Grover Willcox and Kennedy Smartt got Gloria Nabors' address from the card she left at the evangelistic meeting the night before, they went to her apartment, talked with her and with nine-year-old Randy and his sisters about the Gospel, and led them to Christ.[211] When Grover Willcox and Bryant Black saw that Joan McRae went missing from a talk about Christian colleges, they tracked her down at the Peniel Bible Camp swimming pool, and all but forced her to fill out her application to Covenant College.[212] When the mother of four-year-old Gus telephoned Kim Swedlund and told her that she had given up, and was about to drop Gus off at Division of Children and Family Services, Kim jumped in the car and raced over to the mother's house to intercept Gus and bring him into her home.[213] It's safe to say that if we could hear the stories of each Christian presently involved in a New City church, there would be that time or those times when that person was "collared," one way or another, by someone who thought it was important enough, who cared enough, to keep track.

Isn't that what church planting and church growth are all about? Isn't that what the *church* is all about? We are thrilled, and rightly so, when our sanctuaries are full; when we have to go to two services in order to accommodate all the visitors; when we have to close down the registration desk because there are too many applicants for the seats available at a seminar on cross-cultural ministries; when 80 churches have signed up already as participants in New City Network; when the General Assembly overwhelmingly adopts Overture 43. Those results, when we see them, are visible answers to our prayers. They are indeed encouraging, exciting and worthy of our joy and thanksgiving.

---

[211] See p.42.

[212] See p.42.

[213] See p.110.

But we also need to remind ourselves that the heart and soul of building Christ's church is taking the time and spending the gas money to go over to ask a little black girl who lives with her mother in the Projects why it was that she wasn't able to come to Sunday School yesterday.

We missed you. The other children were asking about you. Our family isn't complete without you. We love you. You're important to us. You're important to Jesus. You are a very precious stone, one of the stones Jesus needs to finish building his church.

APPENDIX I

CORE VALUES
(*A Layman's Apologetic*)

THE NEW CITY FELLOWSHIP "WORLD," if it can be so characterized, is not a denomination. It is not incorporated, nor is it structured beyond the governments of its individual churches and ministries. In the foregoing chapters, we have described some of the individual churches, their plants and ministries which fall under the New City umbrella. Most churches mentioned are within one denomination, the Presbyterian Church in America, and in that way have a formal ecclesiastical connection. However, there are other churches and ministries outside the PCA which identify as "New City" works, having no ecclesiastical connection with the PCA or with other New City churches.

It's not quite accurate to call New City a "movement" either, like a group of advocates pushing an agenda. Perhaps NCF would best be described as a "coalescence" of those who find themselves having a common gospel interest, but who believe it is right to emphasize and pursue particular goals within the visible church. These distinctives are primary to their ministries and often different from what might be termed the "mainstream" church. It is because of these distinctives that they have connected together in the New City "world."[214]

THE WHOLE COUNSEL OF GOD

Some critics have questioned the theological propriety of any church, in this case New City Fellowship, in stressing some aspects of Christian duty and mission more concertedly than others. Now there is no denying that different emphases exist among churches. Those attending New City Fellowship in Chattanooga, for example, would no doubt hear many more references to biblical racial reconciliation than they'd hear at a church in rural northwest Iowa where the community is largely Dutch, German or Swedish and less likely to be racially diverse.

And it is true that emphasizing some scriptural truths over others can be dangerous. As Charles Spurgeon said, "Indeed, there are times when the exclusive advocacy of certain important truths has the effect of error."[215] The Apostle Paul, summing up his life ministry, told the Ephesian elders: "I testify to you this day that I am innocent of the blood of all, for I did not shrink from declaring to you *the whole counsel of God*."[216] Paul was subject to human weakness and surely had some personal prejudices, but there is no indication that he went off on tangents, preached pet peeves, or rode theological hobby horses. He could testify, near the end of his life, that he had sought to communicate the *whole* of God's revelation, not picking and choosing. And in telling this to the elders at Ephesus, he was clearly implying that

---

[214] See chapter 9, "New City Network."

[215] Spurgeon, Charles Haddon, "Progressive Theology," (as quoted in *The Sword and the Trowel* [1888]), http://www.godrules.net/library/ spurgeon/ NEWspurgeon_n13.htm (accessed September 20, 2018).

[216] Acts 20:27. The *Westminster Confession of Faith* states: "The whole counsel of God concerning all things necessary for his own glory, man's salvation, faith and life, is either expressly set down in Scripture, or by good and necessary consequence may be deduced from Scripture: unto which nothing at any time is to be added, whether by new revelations of the Spirit, or traditions of men." (Ch.1, Sec.6).

that had been his goal, and should be every preacher's goal, to preach the whole gospel—not just select parts of it.

"Exegeting" the Congregation

Nevertheless, Paul and the other apostles did adjust the subject matter of their preaching and teaching to the peculiar needs of their audiences. They did not always emphasize the same gospel truths. They spent time in their studies, but they also spent time on the street. They sized up their audiences and—based on the "whole counsel of God"—spoke to their peculiar problems, prejudices, errors, gifts, neighborhoods and social circumstances. Indeed, it was because they were commissioned to preach the whole counsel of God that they refused to avoid difficult subjects.

It's been observed that preachers need to do two things as they prepare their sermons: not only must they exegete *scripture*,[217] but they must also exegete the *congregation*. Trevin Wax writes:

> Church exegesis has been going on since the New Testament times. The Apostle Paul did not write a series of letters to "the Church" in general. He knew the problems in Corinth, Galatia, and Thessalonica. So based upon the written revelation of God in the Old Testament Scriptures and the revelation of Jesus Christ, the Living Word, Paul wrote particular letters to particular churches. Why should our messages be any different?[218]

In case there is any doubt about Wax's observation, Revelation chapters 2 and 3 make it clear. Here the Risen Lord himself exegetes seven different individual churches. He identifies them by

---

[217] "Exegete" means to "interpret" or "explain," particularly with regard to scripture.

[218] Wax, Trevin, "Dear Pastor, Please Exegete Your Church." https://www.thegospelcoalition.org/blogs/trevin-wax/pastors-please-exegete-your-church/ (accessed September 20, 2018).

name, specifies their strengths and weaknesses, and tells each of them what they must continue doing, what they must stop doing, and what they must change. He says different things to each of them. All of this Christ bases on his gospel, which by its very nature (because he said it) is the whole counsel of God. It is a divine pattern for the preaching of the Word.

Every church is missioned to preach the gospel in its fullness as revealed in the Bible. And in doing so, the preacher cannot preach wearing a blindfold, nor even an eye patch to see only half the picture. In his messages to the seven churches recorded in Revelation, Jesus is removing blindfolds. To all but two, Smyrna and Philadelphia, he identifies sin and blindness in very particular areas, commands repentance and redirects them in accordance with the truth of his gospel.

Randy Nabors' Exegesis of the Church

The Lord has used Randy Nabors in a special way to help many in a predominately white church to remove some blindfolds. Appendix 2 of this book is a paper he wrote in 1974 while attending Covenant Seminary. By God's providence, he had been placed in a denomination with exactly zero African-American clergy. He surely had blind spots of his own, as every preacher does, but he could see that the Reformed Presbyterian Church, Evangelical Synod, was neglecting some critical matters.

Yet he spoke to a need not just for 'outreach' to the black community, but also for a fully integrated church. This, he believed, was actually possible, but it would require the removal of some blindfolds. It would also mean the establishment of new churches with new objectives, even new *values*—values arising out of, not at variance with, nor in addition to, the whole counsel of God.

I believe Nabors is doing what Trevin Wax wrote about, because in his 1974 paper Nabors exegetes both scripture and the church.[219] He sees a disparity, a big one, between what the Bible says about race issues and the poor, and what the church was or was not doing about it. He sees this as a chasm to be bridged, but only by the grace of God working through his Word and the Holy Spirit, creating a sea change in attitudes and values.

NCF's Core Values

When Third Street Sunday School started in 1968, no one took the time to write up a set of 'core values.' The people involved in it were too busy beating the pavement, passing out fliers and inviting children to come to the first meeting. People on a mission don't always have time to commit their thinking to written form, but nevertheless, these people did have an idea as to what they wanted to see happen, what they wanted to change. The earliest written record of their objectives is one sheet of paper listing things that needed to be done—finding a place to meet, establishing leadership and other organizational matters.

But it also called for three things that should be placed in the "values" column: (1) establishment of a "mercy" committee; (2) seeking out a full-time black minister, and (3) reaching out to children in the community and their families.[220] These charter priorities were rough-hewn and limited; they would be amplified and polished in the years to come. But they have not changed. They were a seminal vision of what would become two primary, continuing core values of New City Fellowship: the importance of biblical racial reconciliation and reaching out to the poor.

As mentioned, the New City world is networked, but unstructured. Hence there is no published set of 'core values' common to all. But a review of the individual ministries' statements of mission or core values shows great commonality among the

---

[219] Will Barker did the same in 1963 with regard to racial issues existent in the church. See chapter 1, "A Surprise, a Murder and a Sermon."

[220] "Downtown mission work: Some priorities" (1968), included in the historical documents of New City Fellowship Chattanooga. The priorities stated in this document preceded Randy Nabors' arrival in the fall of 1969 (see p.45).

networked ministries and churches. I have reviewed many of the various statements that have been set out in writing, and offer this summary:

1. *Authority of the Bible.* We affirm the Bible as the Word of God, and as such it is our absolute authority in faith and practice. All ministries and goals of New City must arise out of scripture, and where they are shown to be in conflict, they must yield to scripture.[221]

2. *Gospel of Reconciliation.* The gospel is the good news that those who believe are reconciled to God through Christ's atoning work on the cross. God commands us to be reconciled to one another as well, and this is possible only through the same good news.

3. *Racial Reconciliation.* God has not only reconciled us to Himself through Christ but has also made peace possible among the nations through Christ. We are intentional in our efforts to bridge gaps among people of different races, ethnicities and social or economic standing. We seek to model racial reconciliation and thus witness to the power of the gospel which enables us to celebrate the unity we have in diversity. We believe this is not just a present requirement but also God's ultimate promise to the church, where people from every tribe, tongue and nation will worship him as one church in heaven.

4. *Outreach to the Poor.* We believe that poverty in society is a result of the curse brought about by Adam's first sin. It is further exacerbated when we neglect or exploit the poor. We believe a central duty of the church is to reach out to and identify with those who

---

[221] New City churches and ministries within the Presbyterian Church in America and the Orthodox Presbyterian Church also accept the Westminster Standards in matters of faith, practice, doctrine and church government, subject to the authority of scripture.

are poor, and that our identification with the poor and helping them in their distress is a primary means of demonstrating the love of Christ to the world. Our ultimate objective in doing so is that all might come to repentance and new life in Jesus as their Savior.

5. *Joyful Worship and Preaching of the Word.* The gospel moves us to worship God with great joy. Believers are to join hands across social and ethnic barriers and lift their voices together in praise. We strive for vibrant, celebrative worship, using a variety of musical styles, with clear, focused preaching from the Word of God.

6. *Children of God.* We believe that when we are saved we become God's sons and daughters, and as such have inherited and continue to inherit his gifts. Believers, as God's children, all have equal standing before him, and are both obligated and privileged to take part in his Kingdom work on earth.

7. *Certainty of God's Covenant Promises.* We believe that God has promised to build his people and his Church in righteousness and to perfection. His promise to do so is absolute and unchangeable, and will not be frustrated. He has chosen to use us in accomplishing this, and his righteousness comes to expression through us as his sons and daughters.

8. *By Grace Alone.* We emphasize the need for God's grace not only in salvation, but also as the only means and power for obedience. We cannot accomplish any of our duties and objectives without a daily dependence on his grace, which is sufficient for our needs and is the only means of our obedience to him.

APPENDIX II

IS AN INTEGRATED CHURCH POSSIBLE?

A POSITION PAPER BY RANDY NABORS (1974)

Biblical material on integration and racism

Genesis 1:26-28; 9:7; 10:25-27 (no distinction made by God between men); 11:1-9 (people scattered because of pride)

Numbers 12:1-15

Matthew 8:11; 28:19-20 (the Great Commission)

Acts 13:1 (an integrated church?); 17:26

Romans 2:9-11

Galatians 3:26-29

Ephesians 2:11-22

Colossians 3:10-11; 3:25 (no respecter of persons)

1 Peter 2:9-10

Revelation 5:9

AMERICA HAS COME THROUGH MANY DIFFICULT DAYS, and it seems that as a whole the Christian church has been unaffected. We speak primarily of America's racial history, and the devastating effect it has had on all of its people. Today it still seems to be true that the most segregated hour in America is eleven o'clock Sunday morning. We discuss this issue because to ignore or deny it would only make the problem worse, although it sometimes seems more peaceful to forget that we as people of God are still not what we should be.

Jesus said, "the truth shall make you free." He went on to say that He is the personification of that truth. We therefore, as Christians, must reflect upon the movement of history through the perspective of the dynamic, Living Word of God: that is, Jesus. He is not dead but living, and His authority attests to, and is attested by, the inscripturated word: that is, the Bible. We have then a proper foundation with which to look at history, and society—a foundation which is stable, and dynamic, and relevant to our situation. The Lord of History is our foundation, and our spectacles.

We have therefore to ask several questions: What is our historical situation (that is, our racial and social context)? What does the Bible teach us about dealing with our historical situation? How can we at New City Fellowship be all that the Body of Christ should be for our times?

Here are some thoughts that attempt to reflect on these and other relevant questions.

1. *You cannot treat people like they do not come from somewhere.*

We cannot look at people as if they were just souls and not bodies. We cannot deal with people in a vacuum or in the abstract. Each individual has (a) a personal and family history, (b) a racial and ethnic history, and (c) a social and economic environment. All of these interact, along with a person's spiritual condition, to make him or her what they are. Each person is different. However, there are historical movements or events that have affected whole peoples; therefore, one can speak of a generalized influence on groups of people. To deny this is great error, both Biblically and intellectually.

Those that have an inadequate knowledge of "self" (what factors make them who and what they are in an historical context) are often the worst victims, even without realizing it, of racial oppression. Some of these victims are the loudest protesters of speaking about those factors that make them, and how they are affected by, what they are.

2. *You have to remember that the Devil is involved.*

We do not ignore the activity of the Evil One, who attempts to use history, and his previous activities of oppression, to keep people from coming to freedom in Jesus Christ. He is still at work, and only the truth and death of Jesus Christ can defeat him.

3. *White people as a group are indicted for America's racism.*

We confess that in the history of our country the Indian, Black, Oriental, immigrant, and Jew have all been oppressed at various times and in various ways. The majority race, in our country—specifically white people (some who even have attempted to name themselves Christians)—have consciously enslaved, sold, exploited, raped, murdered, and denied freedom and personhood to people of color. We confess that people of color, especially black people, have been deprived of their human rights.

We admit that although there were some white people who did not engage in this oppression personally (some even struggled to champion the cause of freedom and died in the attempt) that all white people benefited from this system. This was for the simple reason that they could enjoy the benefits of living in a white society, by simply being white. This makes all white people responsible for their actions and attitudes concerning this historical situation. Either white people will be complicit with the system, or they will attempt to change it. There is no neutral ground.

4. *Guilt and responsibility.*

We see a difference between guilt and responsibility. Many people today are in a dilemma about what to do about the racial injustice of the past, and present. Some white people attempt to do things that would assuage their feelings of guilt, often in some very damaging ways. Some of these are paternalism, cause-orientation, pride and despising other people who have not yet come to the same conclusions about history and injustice. Another activity based on guilt can be sexually expressed, allowing oneself to be caught up in sexual relationships that are based on insecurity and the feeling that this kind of openness will lift the charge of racism from the individual. The dilemma can also be seen in white Sunday School teachers and leaders who do not know how to discipline, because they still cannot see black children as real people. Discipline in its proper place and form is an expression of love, not racism. The absence of discipline is a symptom of fear and guilt.

Black people also have very damaging insecurities concerning dealing with white folks. This can run from one extreme to another: from letting oneself get walked on and used, smiling all the time (because they will not admit to the horror of racism). Fear. Hate. And this comes out in many forms. It is the result of smoldering rage, that sometimes is never openly expressed. It can be very destructive to an individual. Sometimes it leads to self-hate. It can result in an inability to be open with white people, on any level. There never is a deep conversation about one's person (that is, one's own struggles and fears and hang-ups), with the "enemy." Sometimes this insecurity results in violence, certainly distrust, occasionally exploitation, either personally, economically or sexually. Maybe the worst is just cold indifference.

There is such a thing as [proper] guilt. God calls it a result of sin. When we sin we *ought* to feel guilty. This is why we have a conscience and the Holy Spirit to convict us. When one thinks or acts in a racist manner, he or she ought to feel guilty. However, we take the position as Christians that there is only one place to deal with guilt, and that is the Cross. Christians do not need to feel guilty about anything, if they are willing to confess their sins and come to Christ for forgiveness. The only proper response to guilt is to be driven back to the Cross where God offered up His own son in our place, as the punishment for all sin. With true repentance, all racist sins can be washed away. But wait a minute!—does that mean the discussion is over? *Hardly!* We come now to the proper attitude, especially for white people. This is summed up in the word *responsibility*.

Past guilt demands responsibility. Zacchaeus was a tax-collector, who was known as a sinner. Jesus told him to come down out of the tree he had climbed to see Jesus, and to go prepare his house, because salvation had come to it that day. But Zacchaeus wasn't through with the result of his repentance. Half of his goods he would give to the poor, and four-fold he would return to any he had taken from. All his guilt was gone, but the people who had become poor due to his wickedness still needed restitution, and they got it. White people, in order not to remain complicit with the effects of racism, must be about the active business of healing those effects. As individuals, when opportunity affords, as citizens with their vote, as members of institutions that need changing. This responsibility is to be carried out with the wisdom that only the Holy Spirit can give. It requires sensibility, humility, the true expression of servanthood that Jesus requires.

Black people need to throw off the burden that Satan would try to hang on their backs. Feeling insecure and inadequate, as if they had committed some sin and their punishment was to be black and poor. A Godly pride is needed here, and an assurance that they have been created in the image of God, that they are beautiful, that they are somebody. Often those black young people who seem to be most proud are not proud at all, just incredibly insecure. Being loud, violent, impolite, rebellious to parents and authority is not Black Pride, it is sin, and it often comes from a fear that somehow nobody will notice me, and worst of all that I will not notice myself. Do not be made to feel guilty for who you are, and do not be so quick to think that you feel no guilt. Evaluate your behavior, ask yourself why you do the things you do, look deep. If the Devil is trying to put you down, tell him you are a child of God, you take second place to no one, that you are seated in heavenly places with Christ, that you are a member of the royal family of God. This confidence will reflect itself in a quiet, strong kind of pride, one that goes deep. You will not have to constantly prove yourself to everybody, because you know who you are, and how much you are worth. Christian pride comes from the knowledge that God thinks you are worthwhile, not from thinking you are better than someone else. It is shown by being able to be a servant, not because you are forced to, but because you love Christ.

5. *Cultures are different.*

We recognize that there are differences in culture. This is something that goes back as far as the Tower of Babel when, as a result of pride, God separated man from man. However, the sinfulness of mankind is so perverse that even until now, man has reacted in his separation by declaring himself to be superior to those from whom he is separated. Because of our different racial and ethnic and social backgrounds, we each have a different flavor, or culture. When cultures encounter each other, the one having the majority of people, or the power, usually declares the minority to be inferior, or wrong. Cultures, as a whole, are not wrong or right (in comparison with each other); they are just different. However, each culture has things in it that are either God-honoring or pagan. Those things that are pagan need to be denounced, or cleaned up, by Christians. Our cultures need to be claimed for Christ, so that the Lord Jesus can be honored with a little of our flavor given [back] to Him.

Black people have a culture, and even variety within that culture; the same is true for white people. These need to be respected, understood, used and developed for the sake of Christ.

It is here that we must understand our historical situation. To consider integration today, or to consider evangelism from one race to the other and to think that both black and white cultures are coming to meet each other without prior experience, is ignorance. When the white culture met the black on the shores of Africa, the white man held a gun, and chains. The white man tried to destroy the culture of the black man, to cut the black man off from his roots. This effort did seriously affect black people as it gave them a complex problem of identity and purpose. But as the white man tried to convince the black man that he was not even a man, his attempt was a failure. The black man carried the memory of Africa with him, and his worth as a human could not be denied. But to deny that black people in this country were not seriously affected (mentally, emotionally, and thus sociologically), would be a great mistake.

As memories of black people trying to whiten their skin, straighten their hair, pinch their noses and lips to make them look white, preferring among themselves shades of the lighter color, one sees evidence of the horrors of racism. We as a church cannot pretend that this did not happen. We cannot merely seek to forget the past, especially as its results still linger. As Christians we deal with the whole man, and know Christ to be sufficient for all of his problems. Christ is capable to deal with this result of sin as well. We do not fear the struggle behind our captain Jesus.

But how do we deal with it? It hurts even to bring it up. In the context of a multi-racial church we must face certain realities. Which culture will dominate? True integration is when cultures come and mix, without one culture having to give up its own identity. Integration in the past meant for black people to give up any identification with being black and simply melt into the white majority, which in reality the white man would not let him do. He was caught in the middle of the white man's dilemma. Act white, think white, pretend white, but you'd better not marry white.

6. *True integration accepts the realities of history.*

We recognize that in today's historical context, integration must bear in mind historical qualifications. The white culture, due to its ability to still protect opportunity for white people, and equip them with education, cultural awareness, and a rewarded drive to succeed, must not be allowed to dominate in a church that professes to be integrating. When we say 'not be allowed to dominate,' it must not even be allowed to assume itself an equal partner, because in our present context it cannot do so. It will only continue to maintain the privilege of resources which racism secured for it, for example, having the money, having the ideas, the organizational and administrative skills, having the contacts, especially in the Evangelical world.

7. *Homogeneous churches grow.*

We recognize that homogeneous churches (churches made up of people who are the same, in some respect) are the ones that grow. Churches that have something, or everything in common, will be able to pull together and grow. A common effort and purpose is essential for growth.

8. *Black people need to hear the radical Gospel, too.*

We recognize the need for the preaching of the whole Gospel in every community, treating people as whole people. We know that black people as well as white people need to be "radicalized" for Christ, in all their world and life view. We know that even among evangelicals those who are in that category seem to be all too few. Often "radical" white preachers will only preach the basics of Christianity to black people, as if they did not need to hear Christ's teachings on wealth, poverty, violence, community, etc.

9. Reformed and Presbyterian churches needed in the black community.

We recognize the need for Biblical churches in the black community, as well as the white. We know that there is an absence of Reformed and Presbyterian churches in the black community. If we feel these to be Biblical for white people, and if we see Reformed theology as the system of teaching presented in the Scriptures, then this teaching must not be denied to the black community.

10. Gospel-preaching black churches, true churches.

We recognize the validity of black churches which do preach the Gospel of Jesus Christ, although not completely consistent with Reformed doctrine. We hold these churches to be in no sense inferior in standing before the Lord, as long as they honor Christ. However, it behooves every Christian to guard and defend, and produce those disciples which follow all the teachings of Christ. Otherwise, why support Reformed doctrines, or Reformed missions?

11. Theological failure of Reformed doctrine.

We recognize the theological failure of Reformed theology to deal with slavery, racism, poverty and oppression. In this regard it has been a failure, and it still is as long as its seminaries, colleges and churches do not apply the Scriptures to these areas which are so openly discussed in Scripture. Its adherents are not, and have not been, taught to analyze the system for this unrighteousness. Where once it denounced the king, and claimed Jesus as rightful monarch, it gave the throne to Americanism and capitalism and plantationism. God forgive us. We see here a lack in Reformed theology that can only be supplied by the exegesis and hermeneutics of a people involved in the struggle of the oppressed. It is true that theology has been done with a cultural bias. Maybe theology can only be done with a cultural perspective, but if this is so, this theology must be done in full awareness of its cultural bias, with humility and able to accept Godly addition. However, Reformed theology still has much to add to the black community.

12. Biblical call for integration.

We believe that God is at work in the world, adding to His Kingdom, over which He reigns. That this Kingdom is to be made up of every tongue, tribe and nation (see Bible notes). That although many of these groups of people are separated by geographical boundaries, some are not. That the ones that are separated are joined in the same Body, that of Christ. That though we have different historical backgrounds, we are one in Christ. However, the teaching in Galatians is that though we have one Savior, Greek does not have to become Jew, and *vice versa*. All must hold to the same teaching of Christ, all must be in subjection to Him, but we can have our cultural differences. But we also believe that the model of God's Kingdom on earth is not one of racially separate congregations, holding to the same doctrine. What does that show of God's reconciliation, or love between brothers? What does that say to the world? The answer is, nothing. Nothing but a model of what the world already is. Are racially and culturally homogeneous churches unbiblical? Only to the extent that they exclude others who need to be discipled, who are not like them.

13. Nothing is too hard for God.

It seems that true integration in these times is impossible with men, but it is not impossible with God. The reality of history does not need to be denied in the application of the Gospel. The Gospel can be "contextualized."

14. Demand for the negation of whiteness as superior or equal.

We accept the fact that for white Christians to be able to join together with black Christians to build a specific local congregation, they must in a very real sense give up their "whiteness." As they cannot change the color of their skin, which would be even a wrong inner desire, they must change the way they think and act. They must be willing, and practicing, aggressively to take a back seat. They must be servant. They must not let their culture dominate.

15. Whiteness an opportunity for servanthood.

It would be wrong for a white person to think that somehow they could be black. That by the way they sing, act, walk, talk or dress, that somehow black people will not recognize them. God makes us what we are, and he does not err. We should be thankful for what God has made us. However, our context defines our opportunity. White people have the opportunity to be servants.

16. Integration defined.

The thing that makes a church integrated in this day and age is when the minority culture is able to freely express itself and grow, without compromise or injury, when those people who have for centuries been forced to take the back seat now have access to all avenues of power and privilege, and are able to lead without being subject to patronization or condescension. And able to do all of this with the presence of people who represent the majority culture.

17. The problem of image.

We recognize the problem of leadership, and image. Who are the models in an integrated church? This obviously depends on the church. In a predominately black congregation, where there are stable black Christian families, the problem of "models" for young people to emulate is not so much a problem. Integration at this time in history probably works better when whites are in a numeric minority, for even if they are acting as servant and allowing black people to lead and their culture to be freely expressed, just the presence of a greater number of whites can be threatening and stifling. However, in a situation where white people are in a black community, trying to build a church and attract black people, and thus they are in a numeric majority, the problem of models is a serious one. If God has truly called these white people to build a church in the black community, and if they are truly seeking to walk with the Holy Spirit, then it can be remembered that nothing is impossible with God. But it sure will take a lot of Grace for the positive to outweigh the negative. If all the models for successful Christian living are white, the subliminal message to black young people is that black people cannot be spiritual, that black people do not know how to have decent families, that only white people really know the Scriptures and can do things correctly. The odds are against an inner-city church that is comprised mostly of white people really making an impact on the black community, except on a service or charity basis. Black children need black models, if for no other reason than that the rest of society is suffering from the destruction of the black family and black manhood, especially on the lower economic urban level. Inwardly, black people are constantly reminded of the social situation, and can deal with it by becoming bitter, or trying to pretend they have no connection with the rest of their race. It is a depressing problem, this in regard to an inner-city church with a white majority.

The reality is often different from the ideal. We have to be faithful and obedient in the situation we find ourselves in. Several wrong strategies and mentalities are sometimes evidenced in an "integrated" situation. One is the token "N—" syndrome. That is, that every time a black person gets saved, or comes into the church, the white people want to throw the mantle of leadership on him or her, without regard to gifts or personal interest, and sometimes without spiritual maturity. They want this person to be the spokesman, or at least to give the false picture that black people are in control. This can be very dangerous, because the Scriptures speak very pointedly about laying hands suddenly on no man. There is the temptation (for the new "leader") to pride, and to have too much power without knowledge. This can lead to disillusionment, for as this person attempts to do or say things that the real power base will not go along with, the end is bitterness and often schism.

Another erroneous strategy is to never trust the "natives" (an exact parallel from the mission field), to never relinquish control of the levers of power, to always be able to find some excuse as to why the people are not ready for control. Again, the result is bitterness, or paternalism, and inevitably schism.

Leadership development is important in any and all church situations, especially mission-type ministries. The goal is an indigenous, self-governing, self-supporting, missionary-sending church. This development must be done in the steady process called discipleship. The teaching of the Scriptures, the growth in a spiritual walk with Christ, and the humility that goes with it are essential for leadership in the Church. The model that must be presented is Christ. The challenge of the particular ministry must constantly be emphasized, the "ideology" must be articulated; that is, what the vision of the fellowship is, what the cultural awareness should be, what defines the very specific and unique place that individual fellowship has.

In articulating this "ideology" in leadership training, it should not be communicated as if all the weight of it is just waiting to be given over to the shoulders of black people. Jesus Christ does not require the services of any particular individual to be a success in being the Savior. When being a co-laborer with God is presented in its correct perspective, there is no room either for pride, or for being crushed. It is a task given to the believer by Grace; it is a privilege, not a right. It is not a privilege given at the discretion of the white man, but of Christ himself. It is not given without the Grace to see it accomplished. This correct perspective can be a safeguard to the destructive mistakes that often accompany the passing of the mantle. We are not in a hurry, except to follow the Holy Spirit. We are not slow in handing over authority and leadership except as the Spirit of God restrains us.

However, the one factor that is essential to bring about "homogeneity" (apart from race or economics) in a congregation is the challenge of the church's specific mission.

18. Integration not impossible.

With the Lord's help, this task is not impossible. There are strategies that can make it work; there is a positive balance that leads to success in trying to establish an integrated church in this period of American history. It is a balance of common sense, knowing the historical context, the cultural dilemma, knowing the Scriptures, being sensitive, and walking with the Holy Spirit. The mandate for an integrated church is there in the Scriptures (see Bible notes). It is not merely an ideal for heaven. If Christ cannot bring men and women together from different racial and cultural groups, in a fellowship that demands interaction, that the world can see, that provides a context for love and servanthood, commitment, and accountability, then Christianity has nothing to say. To point out the failures of the past to reach this ideal is not sufficient to declare it impossible, or unnecessary. The validity of the mandate is Scripture, not experience. And it must be noted that the past is not solely a record of failure. The success stories hardly ever get told. We remember a year of failure over ten years of success. But even if we have only one good year out of ten, it is worth it.

Conclusion

We see the mandate for Scriptural churches in the black community. We see the need to respect those traditional churches that have not lost their commitment to Christ and the Word of God. We see the Biblical importance of Presbyterian government and Reformed theology. We see the tremendous contribution of black theology, that is, that the cause of the oppressed is our own. We need the freedom of worship expressed in some black traditions. In short, we need everything that is good and helpful in our Church.

Has anyone ever seen a local church do all that it should be doing? Has anyone ever seen a local church be all that it perpetually should be? We doubt it. The whole concept of the Body of Christ is one of growing in grace and truth; it is always a struggle. No one ever said that a specific congregation should last forever. None do; they all change after a generation or so. Even if the building has been there for centuries, the congregation changes as people die and are born. We need to see the struggle as part of the success of growing in grace and truth. Can there ever be stability? Granted, what we are all looking for is a fellowship with dynamic, steady saints, who are spreading the Gospel and teaching disciples, and an environment which exhibits love and light, to each other and to the world. Sometimes this seems to be reached, and we need not to waste that time. Usually we all sit around in the glory of grace and truth and fail to get ready for when the Lord may call some of us home, or to other fields of service, or until some of us slip away, God forbid.

But we are trying, always trying, to make the Body of Christ, when it meets together, a time and place of *koinonia*,[222] where the Lord is truly worshiped.

The Lord God is able to bring *koinonia* to an integrated bunch of folks, even if the horrors of sin and racism and slavery, and all kinds of evil oppression in their racial confrontation seem to give every reason in the world to keep them apart. This is the power of the Gospel. We have found peace in the Blood of Christ, and in His Cross the wall of partition has been broken down—the wall that separated Jew and Greek, and all other walls as well.

In summation, integration is a realizable goal and command for the church today. It can only be accomplished in its truest form if it is done facing the realities of the historical and cultural context. That is, it cannot merely be a cultural pluralism where everyone is given a chance to see a parade of cultural forms, at least not between white and black. There is too much cultural

---

[222] Christian fellowship or communion.

oppression with which to deal. Black culture and presence must dominate if at all possible, watching out for the pitfalls of tokenism and undue caution. It requires the commitment of all those involved, with the homogenizing force being that of a common mission. It is a biblical requirement at the very least for all Christians to fight oppression and injustice, to love mercy and walk humbly with the Lord. It takes a special humbling and call of God to commit oneself to such an attempt in an integrated church, especially for black people. It has taken a special humbling for white people as well, and will again, although at present some white folks find integration a means to deal with an uneasy conscience.

We have mentioned the 'homogenizing' force being that of a common mission. This, it seems to me, is the essential point to capture, in order to make an integrated church a reality. A common sense of mission requires "vision." That means being able to foresee what you want to grow to, and how you want to grow to it, as a church.

Some Christians would not view an integrated church as a goal, but if we are to truly be "salt," it seems we must. Some Christians will find it easier to leave and go to the suburbs, some will find it easier to go to ethnically homogeneous churches, which are traditional. Some may wonder, "why make it harder for people to come to Christ? Get them saved first; then deal with their racism!" Do you know what Jesus would say to that? I hope we do not sound presumptuous when we say that we think we know. Everyone who comes to Christ at all, comes to Him repentant, and acknowledges Him as Lord. But we often want others to exclude Christ from lordship over those areas of life in which we are excluding Him, because we are stubborn in our rebellion, and thus make our converts look an awfully lot like ourselves. Why can we not bring people to Christ in the working model of the Kingdom of God?

An integrated church is certainly not the answer to all the problems in the local congregation. If anything, we have shown in this paper that even more problems seem to be on hand. But it is worth it. Oh what addition we make to ourselves, what broadening of our hearts and minds, to be in that brotherly communion with others who are different-looking from ourselves. What deepening of our lives it brings when, facing the injustice done to others, we recognize that we can no longer conveniently run away from it. God grant the grace for us all to meet this challenge.

INDEX

A

Africa Missions With Nations 129
Ailes, Rodney 45
Alcorn State University 14
Alexander, Rodney 45, 46, 63
Alexander, Rosalind 3
All for Jesus, hymn 44
Anderson, Charles 27, 63
Armes, Jack 16, 18

B

Badenoch, Lester and Sally 116
  Director of Training, Harambee, Lester 117
  NCF Chattanooga 117
Baird, James M., Jr. 155, 157, 160
Barker, Nick 46, 47
Barker, William S. 1, 11, 25, 27, 31, 46, 47, 55, 175
Basse, Macklann and Rose 128
  missionaries to Togo, PMI 129
  ordination, Macklann, Togo Presbyterian Church 129
Bates, Suzanne 108
Battle of Lookout Mountain 34
Becker, Bob 147
Belgic Confession 61
Belz, Linda 2
Belz, Mary 37
Bible Songs Hymnal 84
Birmingham, Alabama, riots 60
Black, Bryant 43, 169
Black Nationalists 55
Black Pride 183
Bolyard, Mark 139
Bruce, Taylor 135
Buchanan vs. Warley 13
Buckey, Kim 133

C

Cadwell, Arline Wetzel 1, 22, 34, 36, 38, 167
Calvary Gospel Church 41, 82

Calvin, John 8, 23
Campbell, Sanders 50
Campus Crusade 143
Carlson, Gordon and Ellen 107
Cedline Bible Camp 46
Center for Urban Theological Studies 95
Chappeau, Gerry and Sharie 118
  City Lights 120, 136
  InterVarsity Christian Fellowship ministry 119
Chattanooga Widows Harvest Ministry 68
Chesapeake Reformed Theological Seminary 72, 77, 143
Citizens' Councils 15
Clay, Sandra 3
Community Presbyterian Church, Nairobi 51, 65, 97
Conn, Harvie 94
Core values of NCF 171
Cornell University 11
Covenant College 11, 25, 26, 33, 34, 43, 44, 112, 116
  Chorale 44
  student constiuency at NCF 62
Covenant Theological Seminary 11, 13, 25, 48, 102
  student constituency at NCF 107

D

Davis, Deborah 109
De La Beckwith, Byron 15
Donaldson, Charles 31
Drexler, Jim and Sara 111, 114
Duncan, Ligon 156

E

Eicher, David J. 34
Ellis, Carl 51, 65, 66, 97, 148
Ellis, Elward 47
equal protection 13
Eshe Oluwa 99

Evangelical Presbyterian Church 26
Evers, Medgar 14, 16

F

Fair Housing Act 13
Fellowship House 68
First Baptist Church, Chattanooga 58
First Presbyterian Church, Chattanooga 58
First Presbyterian Church, Jackson, Mississippi 15, 155
First Reformed Presbyterian Church of Lookout Mountain 27, 34, 45, 46, 47, 50, 58, 59

G

Garafolo, Santo 148
Glenwood, New City Fellowship. *See* New City Fellowship Chattanooga
Good Samaritan 18
Gordon, Mark 147
Gornik, Mark R. 94
Grace & Peace Fellowship 62, 73, 106, 113, 146
Grady, Collette 31
Graeber, Christy 71
Green, Paul 68, 70

H

Hamilton Heights 134, 144
Hamm, John 84
Harper, Warren 103
Harvard Divinity School 48
Hatch, Chris 68, 70
Hawkins, Edwin 85
Hazelwood Reformed Presbyterian Church 11, 13, 25
Henning, Ann Filer 66, 93, 103
Henning, Barry 3, 66, 67, 93
  crisis of faith 96
  interim senior pastor, NCF Chattanooga 100, 102
  Lookout Mountain RPC 102
  move to St. Louis 67
  NCF workdays, influence 98
  New City Network 127, 147
  ordination 96
Orthodox Presbyterian Church 96
  St. Louis decision, move 100, 102
  Taylor Wesleyan Methodist Church 93
  Westminster Seminary 93
Higgins, Mike 69, 72
  Redemption Fellowship, Atlanta 70
  South City Church, St. Louis 70
Hinn, Benny 36
Holland, Bryan 64, 91
Hope for the Inner City 68, 70
Howard University 72
Howell, Jack 126
Hubbard, Roy and Emily 131
  Associate Pastor, NCF South 132
  campus minister, Alabama A&M 132
  Louisiana State University 131
  Reformed Theological Seminary 132

I

Inner-City Missions 57, 59
Integration and kingdom theology 188
Interracial marriage 28, 29, 49
InterVarsity Christian Fellowship 87, 118, 119

J

Jackson, Mississippi 15
Jackson, Randy 71
Johns Hopkins University 72
Johnson, Al and Susan 114
  New Covenant Legal Services 137
Jones, Tom 27
Jubilee School 3, 133

K

Kaufmann, Steve 37
Keller, Tim 147
Kellogg, Doreen 59
  NCF logo 61
  The Sanctuary Banners 61
  worship banners 61, 65

Kellogg, Edward 49, 50, 59
  paintings 61
Kennedy, D. James 42
Kingdom-Builders 71
King, Dr. Martin Luther, Jr. 14
  I Have a Dream speech 33
  Lookout Mountain, reference to 33
Kragnes, Theresa 2
Krispin, Bill 95
Ku Klux Klan 14

L

LeCroy, Tim 158
Long, Griff 59
Lookout Mountain 54
Lookout Mountain Presbyterian
  Church 26, 58
Lucas, Sean Michael 15, 156
Lutz, Al 74

M

MacNair, Greg 2
Mastin, David 114
McClellan, Hugh 48
McGee, Jeff 107, 109, 127
McGee, Jo (Harvey) 109
Memorial Presbyterian Church, St.
  Louis 106, 111, 141
Merrit, Jerome and Willa 108, 110
Miller, Jack 96
  Sonship curriculum 97
Mission to North America 51, 109,
  147, 148
Mississippi, University of 14
Mississippi Valley Presbytery
  Pastoral Letter on Racism and the
    Gospel 161
Mitchell, Dave 58
Murphy Blair Community Church 3,
  73, 133, 146
Muutuki, Elfi 110, 140, 141
Muutuki, Joseph 110, 114, 140
  Daystar University, Nairobi 141
  German Theological Seminary 141
  NCF Nairobi 142
  nosebleeds 140
Myles, Tanya 124

Missionary Baptist Church 125
  mother's death 126
Myles, Tony 124
  Associate Pastor, NCFSTL 127
  Church of the Holy Communion
    124
  Covenant Seminary 125
  Knoxville, TN church plant 126
  Reformed theology, influence 126
  Senior Pastor, NCFSTL 127
  University of Missouri St. Louis
    125

N

Nabors, Gloria 41, 42, 169
Nabors, Joan McRae 39, 42, 169
Nabors, Randy 39, 87, 155, 169
  Biola University 44
  call to Chattanooga 50, 63
  chaplain 49, 70
  Coordinator of Urban and Mercy
    Ministries, MNA 51
  Covenant Seminary 48, 63
  Desert Storm 50, 66, 100
  exegesis of the church 174
  installation, NCF Chattanooga 50
  Is an Integrated Church Possible?,
    position paper (1974) (Appendix II) 179
  marriage to Joan McRae 46
  Merciful 39, 41
  Nairobi, mission work 51, 65
  New City Network, establishment
    147
  ordination 50
Nairobi, Kenya 50
National Association for the Advancement of Colored People
  (NAACP) 14, 16
National Presbyterian Missions 21
NCF Fredericksburg 147
Newark, New Jersey 39, 49
New City East Lake 74, 117
  Latino ministry 75
  particularization 75

New City Fellowship Chattanooga 53, 105
   Chattanooga Christian School, move to 65
   Fellowship House 59
   First Sunday Prayer Meeting 79
   GLAD and Community Outreach 80
   installation of Kevin Smith, Glenwood 78
   leadership crisis, 1974 63
   Lighthouse 71
   mercy ministries 81
   missions 80
   Mitchell Avenue, move to 59
   New City Food Pantry Ministry 81
   particularization 50, 64
   purchase of manse, 2007 72
   small group ministry 79
   thirtieth anniversary 72
   Westminster Presbyterian Church, purchase of 66
   widows ministry 68
New City Fellowship South 127
   Chapel for the Exceptional 128
   Christian Friends of New Americans 137
   first worship service, 2003 127
   Grace Avenue property 128
   Hubbard, Roy 131
   immigrants, outreach to 130
New City Fellowship St. Louis 35, 105
   82nd Street property 114, 120
   African outreach 121
   Ashby Road 113
   City Lights 120
   Health Connection 110, 122
   Hodiamont office 105
   immigrants, outreach to 117, 121
   Murphy Blair 106
   particularization 114
   Rayburn Chapel 106, 107
   single moms' ministry 106, 110, 122
   Sonship curriculum 97, 112, 116
   workdays 106, 109, 136
New City Network 52, 127

   current participant ministries 148
   purpose 152
New Covenant Legal Services 137
New Song Community Church 147
Nielson, Niel 77
Nienhuis, Bob and Jan 111, 114

O

Oliver, C. Herbert 60
Orthodox Presbyterian Church 56, 98
Owens, Patsy 68

P

Parker, Mike and Jodi 112, 115
   Associate Pastor, NCFSTL, Mike 113
   Colortown, Jodi 113
   Fellowship of the Lamb 113
   head of diaconal care, Jodi, NCFSTL 113
   The King's College 112
   Westminster Christian Academy, Mike 113
Parkin, Vera 2
Peniel Bible Camp 42, 169
Philadelphia Presbytery 77
Pickett, James 67, 72, 148
   Associate Pastor, NCF Chattanooga 71, 74
   Covenant Seminary experience 73
   installation, New City East Lake 75
   Murphy Blair 73
Pickett, Michele Albury
   Erlanger Hospital, Chattanooga 74
Plummer, Wy 143, 148
   Coordinator of Mission to North America's African-American Ministries 72
   Executive Pastor, NCF Chattanooga 72
Potomac Presbytery 158
Presbyterian Church in America 51, 56, 171
   formation 155
   Overture 43, 2016 158, 163
   Overture 55, 2016 160, 163

Pastoral Letter on Racism and the Gospel, 2016 161
Personal Resolution on Civil Rights Remembrance, 2015 156
racial reconciliation 79
Presbyterian Church in the United States 26
Presbyterian Mission International 129
Princeton University 11

R

Rayburn, Robert G. 44, 48
Redeemer Presbyterian Church 147
Reformed doctrine, theological failure of 187
Reformed Presbyterian Church, Columbus Synod 11, 21
Reformed Presbyterian Church, Evangelical Synod 50, 84, 174
  interracial marriage 29, 49
  Report of the Committee on Racial Questions 29
  Synod of, 1965 27
  Synod of, 1968 28
Reformed Presbyterian Church, General Synod 83
Reformed Presbyterian Church of North America 26, 83
Reformed University Fellowship (RUF) 131
Restore St. Louis 132
  Firm Foundation tutoring 132
  Freedom School 133
  Harambee 117, 134
  Health Connection 135
  InsideOUT Prison Ministry 135
  Umetulisha 137
  Workday 136
restrictive covenant 13
Rice, Tim and Kathy 122
  Congo 123
  St. Louis University School of Medicine 122
  Vanga Evangelical Hospital 123
Richer, Julia 108
Ricks, Peaches 22, 37, 167

Riley, Patricia 45

S

Sanderson, John W. 83
Schaeffer, Francis 73, 83, 129
Schmidt, Collyn 1, 25, 31, 34, 36, 37, 56, 71
Schmidt, Rudolph 1, 25, 31, 35, 45, 48, 49, 50, 78, 168
  death of 71
Sherow, Ron 48
Shuman, Tom 137
Skinner, Tom 54, 65
Smallman, Steve 147
Smartt, Kennedy 42, 43, 86, 157, 169
Smith, Kevin 75
  Boice, James Montgomery 77
  Calvinism 76
  Church of God 75
  Pineland Presbyterian Church, pastor 77
  Senior Pastor, Glenwood 75, 78
  West Oak Lane Church of God 75
Smith, Sandra Brown 76
  Jamaican birth 76
  Roman Catholic Archdiocese of Philadelphia 76
Sola scriptura 30
Songs of the New City 64
Southern Presbyterian Church 27
Southside YMCA 59
Spurgeon, Charles 172
Steele, Leona 109
Stern, Andrew 140
Stewart, Leland 65
St. Louis University 25
St. Pierre, Lisa 138
  Administrative Assistant to pastor 140
St. Pierre, Steve 138
Swedlund, Bryan and Kim 110, 114, 135, 169

T

Third Street Sunday School 1, 10, 22, 31, 34, 45, 46, 53, 55, 57, 59, 78, 86, 144, 167

widows ministry 68
Thompkins, Tony 113, 115
Tower of Babel 184
Trimiew, Oliver 45, 77
Trinity Hymnal 56, 64, 86
Tuinstra, Anna Gallant 131
Twin Oaks Presbyterian Church 120

V

VandenBrink, Kevin and Stephene 129
  Schaeffer Institute, Covenant Seminary 129
  senior pastor, NCF South, Kevin 130

W

Wachsmuth, Dan 114
Wade in the Water 22
Ward, Beth Moore 54, 56, 86
Ward, James C. 2, 56, 57, 83, 108, 123
  Black and Blues Band 85
  Covenant College 84
  Death is Ended 90
  Elan 88
  Highway 88
  InterVarsity 87
  Morning Sun 86
  Mourning to Dancing 88
  musical influences 85
  New York, move to, 1975 64
  Third Street Sunday School 86
  Who Can Separate Us 89
Ward, Jim 107, 123
  missionary, Peru 108
Ward, Kirk 123
Ward, Samuel 83, 90, 124
Wax, Trevin 173
Westminster Confession of Faith 156, 172, 176
Westminster Presbyterian Church 26
Westminster Shorter Catechism 30
Westminster Theological Seminary 11, 60
White, Darwin and Lori 3, 108
Willcox, Grover 42, 43, 47, 169

Williams, James 126
Williams, Marvin 70
Williams, Thurman 142, 148
  Chesapeake Theological Seminary 143
  Faith Christian Fellowship, Baltimore 142
  Grace & Peace Fellowship 143
  New Song Community Church, pastor 143
Work, John Wesley (II) 21
World Presbyterian Mission 21, 50
Wycliffe Bible Translators 131

Y

Yarborough, Bill 121, 127
Yarbrough, Angie 134
Yarbrough, Michael 134
Young, John M.L. 83
Young Life 142

EVERY PRECIOUS STONE

Made in the USA
Columbia, SC
30 December 2018